CLOSE TO OUR HEARTS

Personal Reflections on Marriage

edited by

Aldegonde Brenninkmeijer-Werhahn
and
Klaus Demmer

LIT

Cover image: Salvatore Sciascia, 2000 (private collection INTAMS)

Bibliographic information published by the Deutsche Nationalbibliothek
The Deutsche Nationalbibliothek lists this publication in the Deutsche Nationalbibliografie; detailed bibliographic data are available on the Internet at http://dnb.d-nb.de.

ISBN 978-3-643-90339-6

A catalogue record for this book is available from the British Library

Klosbachstr. 107
CH-8032 Zürich
Tel. +41 (0) 44-251 75 05
Fax +41 (0) 44-251 75 06
E-Mail: zuerich@lit-verlag.ch
http://www.lit-verlag.ch

LIT VERLAG Dr. W. Hopf
Berlin 2013
Fresnostr. 2
D-48159 Münster
Tel. +49 (0) 2 51-62 03 20
Fax +49 (0) 2 51-23 19 72
E-Mail: lit@lit-verlag.de
http://www.lit-verlag.de

Distribution:
In Germany: LIT Verlag Fresnostr. 2, D-48159 Münster
Tel. +49 (0) 2 51-620 32 22, Fax +49 (0) 2 51-922 60 99, E-mail: vertrieb@lit-verlag.de

In Austria: Medienlogistik Pichler-ÖBZ, e-mail: mlo@medien-logistik.at
In Switzerland: B + M Buch- und Medienvertrieb, e-mail: order@buch-medien.ch
In the UK: Global Book Marketing, e-mail: mo@centralbooks.com
In North America: International Specialized Book Services, e-mail: orders@isbs.com
e-books are available at www.litwebshop.de

Table of Contents

Theological Focal Points

Anthropology of Marriage

Paths to Maturity in Marriage

Biographical Perspectives and Experiences

Preface

Aldegonde Brenninkmeijer-Werhahn

I recently went for a long walk with my nephew. Our conversation touched on many topics and was very stimulating. We also talked about the present book. What is the point of yet another book about marriage, when there are already so many publications on this topic? Do young people and young married couples today no longer have any need of lived testimonies about how a marriage can be successful? Young and old are surrounded nowadays by family members and friends who have experienced the painful separation of their parents, siblings, or couples with whom they are friends. Or else they have experienced in their own lives the breakup of a relationship. Is it then surprising that the faith in a healthy emotional security is shattered, and that our society is increasingly characterized by a fear of commitment?

My nephew's questions gave me food for thought. It was important for this young man as well to get pointers on how married life can succeed and can come to maturity over the course of time. No one is helped by cheap "do it yourself" recipes or by trivial and vacuous love-stories. Rather, what is needed here, as everywhere else in life, is the willingness to learn values, to practice virtues, and to open oneself to faith experiences. But do we married people have the courage, and do we take the time required,

to listen genuinely and to open up in a discreet manner, so that we communicate the treasure of our experience of marriage and our insights into life in a way that is unobtrusive, authentic, and sensitive, without infringing upon the freedom and dignity of the other person? The young generation – but also society as a whole that is getting older and older – is searching desperately for testimonies, practical guidance, and points of orientation in order to shape a model for their own lives, to maintain a steady course, and if necessary, to undertake course corrections.

When INTAMS (International Academy for Marital Spirituality) was founded in 1989, it could certainly not be taken for granted that an international group of independently thinking married laypersons and celibates would come together to devote themselves in full seriousness and with great honesty to the study of unresolved questions about the marital partnership. Their goal and intention was, first of all, to devote their entire attention to marriage. The central issue that determined our work was not the fear of marital breakdown, but rather the question why so many marriages still succeed, and what influence successful marriages have on the start of a family and on the education of the children. As well, we were interested in the question of the effect this has on the social, political, and cultural environment. Finally, we wanted to look closely at the unhappy marriages. This prompted us to seek to develop a spirituality of marriage in its entire spectrum. We became ever more aware that the demands that are made of marriage are high, and that the most helpful thing would be a sensitive accompaniment by married couples. We understood our academic work not only as providing help in the social, political, and cultural sphere, but above all as also a service of the Church. The Church owes married couples a service of this kind, if it truly intends to share in responsibility for marriage and married life. The intention was to reflect, research, publish, and communicate

in a manner that united the Christian confessions. The work was to be interdisciplinary and to have both an academic and a practical pastoral orientation. The present book aims to show something of the work we have carried out in common over the past two decades. The articles are not homogeneous. Their aim is to invite the reader to choose one or other article that can provide stimulus. This means that not every article will appeal equally to the reader. The authors have collaborated for many years. They have accompanied this initiative with their sympathy and their active support. This book draws both on their academic resources and on their practical experience of life. It seeks to illustrate the value and the difficulties of a lifelong relationship in its various facets, and to hand on something of this to the coming generations, as it were from heart to heart.

The authors approach the relationship of married life in five movements. The German moral theologian Klaus Demmer introduces the subject in his essay on *Sacramental Marriage – A Testimony of Faith in a Secular World*, by investigating the significance and the depth of the sacrament of marriage. He develops a theology of marriage that is clearly aware of its debt to the Second Vatican Council. On the basis of the biblical idea of covenant, the sacrament of marriage appears here like a beacon in the opaqueness of our time and in the daily lived reality of a relationship.

In the first section, *Theological Focal Points*, the Belgian Cardinal Godfried Danneels likewise takes his starting point in the Council. With reference to the shared Jewish and Christian tradition, he presents the family as a domestic church and indicates the significance of its "domestic liturgy," which has largely been forgotten. It is not commandments and prohibitions that define a marriage, but growing into a domestic spirituality.

The German dogmatic theologian Gisbert Greshake describes the spirituality of marriage on the basis of the triune God, as com-

munio, an exchange of life and of love. It is precisely in being different that the divine Persons and therefore also the marriage partners achieve their unity. Their love is realized in the rhythm of giving – receiving – and giving back. This means that the play of love that takes place between the Persons takes the form of loving, being loved, and "loving with."

The Anglican theologian Adrian Thatcher emphasizes an additional aspect here, namely, that there is also an erotic dimension in the relationship of love of the triune God. The Trinitarian love allows us to experience what it means to be the source of joy for each other, to give and to receive in joy. And the child, as the "other" of the relationship between two persons, is given its place in this way.

In the Christian liturgy of matrimony, the partners promise each other lasting fidelity "for better for worse, in sickness and in health, till death do us part." Does this not mean, therefore, that the relationship of love also includes the yearning for eternity? The German-Belgian theologian Thomas Knieps-Port le Roi shows us how the "love for life" also includes, in a painful way, the death of one's married partner.

The Dutch dogmatic theologian Herwi Rikhof reflects on marriage as a sacrament. He takes his starting point in Ian McEwan's short story *On Chesil Beach*. In his article *Love and Patience*, he describes the significance of the marital covenant and leads us from the New Testament to the tradition of a Trinitarian theology in which marriage and Church equally have their place.

In the second section, on *Anthropology of Marriage*, the Irish moral theologian Enda McDonagh shows us there is always a tension in friendship and intimacy between familiarity and strangeness. Sometimes, one knows one's own self very little, and the partner or friend can be just as alien.

The German theologian Ulrich Dickmann also emphasizes the

complexity of marital love in his article *The Beloved Remains the Other*. With his starting point in E. Levinas, he shows that eros plays a role in the relationship to transcendence, and that it can provide fruitful inspiration for a spirituality of marriage.

The French married couple Jacqueline and Alain de Layre describe in their article *Marriage, a Sacrament for the Road* the advice that parents can give their children who are waiting to get married. Every marriage is unique: therefore love, friendship, and sexuality must be rediscovered and renewed again and again.

The American theologian David Dawson Vásquez describes marriage from a theological perspective as a movement between suffering and resurrection. Not only joys are shared with each other: the otherness of one's partner must be discovered, endured, and accepted.

The sociologist Giulia Paolo Di Nicola and the philosopher Attilio Danese from Italy reflect on the fruitfulness of the marital relationship and identify many other dimensions in addition to the biological procreative power. They look at professional work and societal, political, or cultural involvement, as well as religiosity.

In the section on *Paths to Maturity in Marriage*, the Italian moral theologian Carlo Rocchetta shows in his essay *Crisis in a Couple – How Can one Salvage a Relationship?* how important it is to find the right partner. Even more importantly, however, one must become a suitable married partner. This is the fruit of his observation after many years of accompanying couples.

The Belgian theologian Ilse Cornu describes the path to maturity in a marriage between the *mysterium fascinosum* and *tremendum*. In her article *A Gift for Life*, she draws our attention to the various situations and emotional elements to which married partners are exposed. These include vulnerability and limitation, as well as the abiding search for the "perfect" partner. Do not realism and level-headedness often fall by the wayside here?

From the perspective of pastoral theology, Annette Barker from London writes about everyday life in marriage. Is it possible to speak about the mystery of marriage even in the everyday life of a relationship – as Saint Paul does in the Letter to the Ephesians? And how does one recognize that God's love is at work even in everyday living?

Married people experience in their shared life various phases and paths of maturity. This also applies to sexuality. The Belgian sexologist Alfons Vansteenwegen describes how variously the partners can experience sexual intimacy. The fascinating question here is how, against this background, it is possible for common elements to emerge. Therapeutic praxis shows that a sexuality experienced in common also needs time.

We are increasingly challenged by the inexorable process of getting older. In her article *The Art of Growing Old*, Aldegonde Brenninkmeijer-Werhahn describes various phases of maturity that are experienced precisely by an elderly person. The increased life expectancy presents a special challenge in this context. What does it mean, against this background, to make the marriage vow "till death do us part"?

The final section of the book looks at *Biographical Perspectives and Experiences*. The British psychoanalyst Jack Dominian draws on his decades of therapeutic praxis with couples and on his own marriage with his deceased wife Edith. He reveals to the reader how rich a Christian marriage with its various phases in life can be. His experience teaches him that despite the cares of everyday life and the ever-recurring incalculabilities, it is possible to recall the original love.

Another important aspect, which is often forgotten in the theological reflection on Christian marriage, concerns the married priests. The Italian priest and professor Basilio Petrà, who is equally at home in the Orthodox and the Roman Catholic tra-

ditions, studies them in his article *The Theological Value of the Married Priesthood*. The ministerial priesthood of the Western Church is normally linked to the obligation to celibacy. Despite his celibate way of life, the priest, like the baptized layperson, lives out his spiritual vocation completely in the world. In the Orthodox Church, on the other hand, the celibate way of life is linked only to the vocation to monasticism. This sheds a new light on the union between God and his people that Paul describes in the Letter to the Ephesians.

The English pastoral theologian Elizabeth Davies examines in her article the ability and the necessity to school oneself in perseverance, especially when blows of fate and crises bring married life out of its equilibrium. She writes that even one whose marriage ends in shipwreck can preserve and develop the ability to become a person who loves more and more.

How can a marriage be lived honestly? The American-Italian married couple Elvira Roncalli (a philosopher) and John Ries (a theologian) look at this question. How does one demolish unnecessary façades that one has built up over against the other? And how does one detach oneself from ideals about how one's partner ought to be? According to the authors, marriage is a life's work that does not come into being automatically, but requires continual change and new orientation. This explains their title: *Married Life: A "Revolutionary Road"?*.

The American theologian Donna Orsuto shows in her article *John Henry Newman on Marriage and Family Life as a School of Love* how helpful and important well-prepared Sunday sermons are for married couples and their families. She takes John Henry Newman's sermon "Love of Relations and Friends" as a model and shows us the significance of marriage as a school of love. When one bears in mind how many different personalities live

together in a family, one sees that it is the place par excellence where intimacy, friendship, and love of neighbor can be practiced.

The title of this book was chosen consciously. The essays are meant to be an encouragement for many "experienced" married couples, but also for those who consider getting married. At the same time, this book wants to give hope and glimpses of light for all marriages, even those that are not successful.

Beginning a serious conversation entails a risk. This book undertakes the risky attempt to open up from heart to heart. In addition, I hope that it can also offer pointers on urgent questions such as sexual morality, interchurch marriages, or the problems connected with divorced and remarried persons. It is not prohibitions that solve the problems, but only the path of following Christ, as Saint Paul writes in his Letter to the Galatians: "Carry each other's burdens" (Gal 6:2).

In conclusion, I should like to thank Professor Klaus Demmer, who was present at the inception of INTAMS and has given me his active support for twenty-five years. I am also very grateful to all those who have made their generous contributions to the present book. We recall with great gratitude Cardinal Carlo Maria Martini, a great church leader and prophet for the worldwide church, who went to his eternal home with God our Father on August 31, 2012. He never tired of reminding me of this book again and again. Together with Cardinal Godfried Danneels, he courageously and generously supported the lay initiative of INTAMS until his death. I am grateful to Thomas Knieps-Port le Roi for the fruitful years in which I have been permitted to work closely together with him. I am grateful to Dominique van Haelst for her untiring help in making possible the publication of this book. I thank Brian McNeil and Jenny Besselsen who have done a professional job in translating these texts from several languages into English. I am very grateful to my nephews Konstantin, Alexander,

and Ferdinand, who have helped me greatly through their critical questions.

I am particularly grateful to my husband Hubert. He encouraged me, strengthened my resolve, and supported me in the foundation of INTAMS, even when quiet domestic life sometimes drew the shorter straw as a result. The twenty-five years of work with INTAMS have taught both of us the virtue of perseverance. We are grateful for this, and we do not wish to remain silent about this experience.

Finally, with complete human confidence, I address you, unknown reader, and I wish you many good hours of reading and enriching conversations with your married partner.

Aldegonde Brenninkmeijer-Werhahn
Brussels – Sint-Genesius-Rode
8 September, 2012

Sacramental Marriage – A Testimony of Faith in a Secular World

Klaus Demmer

Impulses from the Contemporary Context

More and more people are coming to accept the insight that theological reflection is biographically "earthed." In his thinking, the theologian takes responsibility for his own life story. He engages in theology from the perspective of a unique and distinctive "I." And he assumes implicitly that what he thinks will find its echo – no matter how nuanced this may be – in the thinking of other persons. He does not stand alone: his interior world can be communicated, and it can receive impulses from the outside. In his thinking, the theologian also takes responsibility for his own time. He is like a highly sensitive seismograph that can register even the slightest vibrations before these reach a wide public. But he cannot be tied down to the role of the passive observer. He also wants to shape things actively and to change circumstances. For the Church has commissioned him to think.

It is in this perspective that my own reflection on marriage is located. It can easily be seen that today, unlike the situation in earlier times, the path to marriage lies open to everyone. Marriage resists the pressure to innovate. Nevertheless, one can no longer

speak of a monopoly, since marriage must share the sphere of public societal life with variants, and these can count on a wide acceptance. People often lack the courage and the willingness to commit themselves to an irrevocable decision that accepts responsibility for itself as such in the public sphere. The term "fear of commitment" was coined and became widespread. I realized increasingly that a pastoral crisis existed here, with its roots in a human crisis, but also in a societal crisis. It was necessary to track this down and to pursue paths of healing from the root.

It was thus necessary to have confidential conversations with those who were immediately affected, that is to say, with committed married couples. The theologian came to see clearly how the vital contact to the societal context has changed. Many of our contemporaries live in an understandable attitude of putting up barriers against a public sphere that they experience as aggressive and imposing regulations on them. They insist on the freedom to form the most intimate and vulnerable areas of life. They construct their "little world," in which it is still possible for originality and spontaneity to succeed. This is why the appropriate reaction on the part of the theologian is not an over-hasty moralization and suspicion. The tone of the theologian's comments should be dictated by understanding.

In the course of my own biography, I have also become aware that in our "knowledge society," the solid knowledge of the faith has remained hopelessly underdeveloped. This hard fact is one of the wounds of the church. An intellectual helplessness is spreading among many Christians, even among those who are educated. This affects fundamental truths of the faith. In a world that elevates factual knowledge to its reserve currency, the necessary soil on which existential decisions based on the faith can grow is washed away. This meant that I was confronted by the challenge of elaborating a theology of marriage that comes from the

heart of the Church. This theology must be borne by insight and permeated by experience. Academic standards and "grass-root" theology should coalesce to form a symbiosis. It was necessary to find a platform on which both married and unmarried persons could make their specific contributions.

Pluralization and globalization leach the identity of a Christian existential world that has grown in the course of time. This is a creeping process. The intellectual horizon is indeed widened, but this takes place at the cost of depth – and the consequence is an intellectual uprooting. We must therefore have the courage to aim at excellence. The power of the Christian idea of God must be allowed to speak. One who wants to withstand the pressure to level things down must live out of the fascination of a vocation that mobilizes the best forces, and out of a reality that is greater than one's own self and that survives one's own death. This means that we need strong personalities, since only they are capable of keeping alive the lofty cultural achievement that is the institution of marriage. These must be people whose life is embraced by an existential task. It thus appeared to me obvious that one must bring together the theology of the sacrament of marriage and a theology of vocation: these are two sides of the same coin. To take this as my starting point seemed to be an urgent and rewarding task. One may indeed speak of a "trademark" that from then on would characterize the work of INTAMS (International Academy for Marital Spirituality).

Interdisciplinary Openness

Throughout my life, I have regarded it as axiomatic that theology can be done only at the point of intersection with other sciences. The theologian must not be afraid of such contacts. His closeness

to life must be guaranteed. This is a question of intellectual culture: it is a simple matter of fact that thinking today is networked.

The founding generation held that INTAMS could be a kind of laboratory for theological reflection and exchange about marriage. Progress in insight is possible only where people's dealings with each other are marked by a trustful dialogue. It was thus necessary to put out feelers in search of contributions, especially from sociology and psychology, without however giving rise to the suspicion of a blinkered mentality. The only criterion was professional competence. Similarly, a person's background in a religious confession or worldview may not play any role. The guiding conviction of all the founders was that one who makes lofty theological claims must know the sphere of human conditions, for only so can the surplus value of theological thinking meet and form the existential reality of the human person.

But where was the theologian to begin, when his theme was marriage as a sacrament, that is to say, in the horizon of faith? All he could do was to take the bull by the horns – more precisely, to begin with the most urgent problem of the present day, the question about God, and to see in this question the vertex of sacramental theology. This is the highest challenge to thought in a profane milieu, since all the truths of the faith are transparent to this question, and must therefore be reflected upon in the light of this question. There is a creeping tendency to understand the sacramental celebration of marriage as at most an ecclesiastical extra. No doubt, God's blessing is invoked upon the marriage – but what is this understood to mean? Is there a consciousness of the undiminished power of the Christian idea of God, of the revolutionary reshaping and reinterpretation of all reality through God's incarnation?

My primary personal concern was to understand the indissolubility of marriage not as an oppressive demand, but as an exis-

tential task full of promise, a task at which one works for a whole lifetime. Married people are *en route* with a promise. They look at one another by looking in the same direction. As friends of God, they cultivate the gift of friendship with one another. In order for this to succeed, INTAMS was to offer a forum that makes available the necessary help for thinking and working.

Dealing with Failure in a Reconciliatory Way

The indissolubility of sacramentally contracted marriage is a burdensome, unreasonable demand not only for the dominant zeitgeist, but also for many committed Christians. This can easily be observed by anyone who looks around his or her world with alert eyes. Marriages can fail in a wholly undramatic manner, and those involved just get on with their lives. Indeed, people can make themselves secure by including the possibility of failure in their calculations, and allowing the marriage to fail can become an option with which one had already (though only secretly) reckoned. Failure had been integrated surreptitiously into the planning of one's life. But my own milieu, priestly and religious life, offered depressing examples too. Biographies that began with a lofty commitment took a sudden end. Guilt and fate seemed inseparably intertwined. This was a salutary impulse that prompted me to reflect on the success and failure of life stories.

But how could this impulse be translated into action? Collaboration with psychologists and sociologists uncovered a great variety of nuances in the word "failure." There are completely undramatic types of failure: it proves impossible to realize individual goals or wishes, because unpropitious circumstances move towards their own contrary goals with a power greater than even the best will, and people do not possess the living skills that are required, if one is to deal strategically with this experience. They

have to learn that not everything in life is equally important and urgent. Living skills include the ability to postpone one's wishes and to bid farewell to them. One must make the best of the remaining possibilities – this is a question of compensation. Besides this, every mature human being and Christian is aware that he possesses the totality only in a fragment. He comes to rest objectively in a realistic measure of self-realization.

I also found the contact with sociology enlightening. It is not wrong to speak of a detraditionalization of society, which corrodes the stability of life partnerships. Under such circumstances, it is extremely difficult to make one's plans with certainty. Role models in society become liquid. This makes the tension between the personal identity (which the existential decision to marry promises one) and the societal milieu of this identity more and more precarious. There are many identities under the sheltering roof of the unique existential choice, and this is both a burden and an opportunity. This opened up a field of work for INTAMS: How can the Christian *qua* Christian survive this challenge?

As time went on, I realized that it was necessary to reflect on a theology of vocation in an anthropological and ecclesiological perspective. It was necessary to create an awareness of this lofty claim. I was convinced that only an honest culture of communication between partners is capable of holding together life worlds that are drifting apart, of overcoming the alienations that necessarily occur, and of reserving the necessary "prime time." It is the task of believing marriage partners to manage the continuous balance between gain and loss that accompanies an existential bond throughout one's life. Lasting help for marriages that are in a crisis can come only from married couples themselves, since the Church is constructed from the bottom up. Often, there are great married couples who are like navigational lights. They have an equal place alongside the existential witness of the unmarried

Christian. There are numerous examples from Church history, not least from periods of persecution and resistance. Besides this, the theology of marriage offers a welcome opportunity to reflect on women's position and role in the Church. What we need is the presence of the educated and self-aware woman. Women ought to show that Christianity is an educational event of unique rank.

The Church as an institution offers the protective framework for a pilgrimage of the spirit. It is a fellowship of the spirit in solidarity, and it is the immediate living sphere of theological thinking: theology lives from the spiritual treasures of many successful life stories. My own biography has taught me well that closeness and partnership along the way are the "first help" that allows one to grow into ever larger spheres of freedom and certainty. The courage to accept the transitory prepares the ground for the definitive.

Theological Focal Points

The Christian Family as "Domestic Church"

Godfried Cardinal Danneels

A *Domestic Church*

One hears it frequently: if the Church speaks about the family, then one only hears references, commandments and prohibitions relating to morality. Once in a while a little bit of dogmatic theology with reference to the sacrament of marriage. But one hears so little about spirituality in marriage, prayer and liturgy in the family. In *Familiaris Consortio* (FC), published after the synod on the family (1981), one finds nonetheless a curious new name for the family: the *domestic church*. Later, in the *Catechism of the Catholic Church* (CCC), this is worked out in detail (1635-1658). It was actually already mentioned by Vatican II (*Lumen Gentium* (LG) 11). But this idea was not explored in depth until the synod of 1980, dedicated to the family. The fact that the family may be called a *domestic church*, means that whatever can be said of the larger Church, can, *mutatis mutandis*, also be said of the Christian family.

This means consequently that the parents are also the first proclaimers of faith and the first "priests" to preside in the family service of worship. They preside also in the "service in miniature,"

the service to children and society. Evangelizing, celebrating and serving are thus etched deeply on the heart of the Christian family.

The family is the privileged place, where the priesthood, received through baptism, is practiced by the father, mother, children and all members of the family: through the reception of the sacraments, through prayer and thanksgiving, through the witness of a holy life, and through active charity (LG10). As a result, the *domestic church* is the first school of the Christian life and the primary place for growth to deeper humanity (*Gaudium et Spes* (GS), 52). Here one learns endurance and the joy of work, the generous, yes even repeated forgiveness, and above all, the divine worship of prayer, and of the sacrificing of one's life (CCC 1657).

The Proclamation in the *Domestic Church*

The mandate of proclamation that the parents have received, applies in the first place in relation to their own children. But in actual fact, it also relates to the father and mother: they evangelize each other. Even more than this, the children are also evangelists: they catechize their parents.

Sometimes you hear it said that fathers and mothers do not have the right to determine the path that a child, at such a young age, should follow – that then of faith – and that children have not been able to choose for themselves. Early religious education would then be an exploitation that takes place on land one does not own. Would it then not be better to apply a time of waiting or a moratorium? Or as Tertullian put it: "Let the children come to Christ when they have grown up."

It is certainly true that no-one has the right to force something on another, not even on one's own child. But, on the other hand, does not everyone have the duty of introducing another to what is good, and certainly his own child? And is it really true that who-

ever dares to feed his child dogmatic certainties, actually slows down his development? And is it really true that if you offer certainties to your child before he inquires about them himself, you slow down a child's mental development and nip it in the bud? The mind, it is said, only begins to work when it has previously had to wrestle with questions. And are these not neutralized by an early religious upbringing?

This reservation may seem reasonable, modern, and a testimony of respect toward the other. But is it really the case that the introduction of faith neutralizes critical questions? Does faith not awaken as many questions as it answers? Is a child – or whoever – capable for that matter of living without initial certainties? The choice between either solid dogmas and fixed moral teaching, or free inquiry, is not a child's dilemma.

Can a child cross the road safely without a zebra-crossing? Or should it just step out into the chaos of traffic? This also applies to the worlds of ideas and religion. It is better to have a place where one is anchored, where serenity and safety are experienced, and to be able to ask critical questions about life from this environment.

Children have Rights

Children have rights. Of course! The right to be born, fed, and educated, the right to medical care and education, the right to grow, to be respected and to intimacy. But they also have the right to intellectual formation, to moral development and to become fully human. They have the right to receive explanation about nature and the world, about society and about humanity. Why then not also: the right to hear about God? Children are naturally inquisitive and contemplative. If initially the religious world and the world of fairy tales overlap, this is not something to be worried about. Corrections will take place spontaneously later on. But it

is important that children have been given the opportunity to develop their ability to sense the mystery, and that they have been initiated into the world of "wonder."

The Bible and the Icons

Children need time to grow. Gratitude and love develop slowly and this requires time. There are however two domains in which the child possesses an uncanny talent that seems to be mature right from the start: the memory and the imagination. A child remembers everything (and with the heart!) and effortlessly registers thousands of images. It is precisely because of this that the *domestic church* has the task of feeding and nurturing the child.

In the first place, there is the nurturing of the memory of the heart. The Bible is especially valuable in this context. Children are made to listen to the Bible. It is, so to speak, written in their language: beyond logic, full of stories, and crammed with symbols, a mixture of epic, poetry, lessons of life and prayer. Every catechist knows how freshly and spontaneously children can respond to Bible stories and what surprising conclusions they often immediately draw. Many people maintain lively memories throughout their lives of the biblical history they were taught at primary school.

A considerable number of children nowadays have an injured imagination. It is in this area that they require the most healing. Countless images of aggression, violence and eroticism are imprinted on their retina. Their image archive is impaired. For this reason, alternative illustrative material is needed for children. And this is something the *domestic church* can provide: beautifully illustrated children's Bibles for reading aloud, the comic strips about the saints, the daily bedtime story from a children's picture book before going to sleep.

In addition to this is the healing effect brought about by looking at icons. One cannot exactly call icons "beautiful": they are often anatomically inaccurate and the look in their eyes is always very serious, not one of childlike affection. Neither do they have anything of the sumptuous splendor of the velvet and silk panels of the Flemish primitives of the Middle Ages. And yet children will gaze with fascination at icons. Perhaps because a Madonna of Van Eyck says: "Look at me, see how beautiful I am." But an icon of Mary says: "I look at you, you are even more beautiful!"

The Domestic Liturgy

Jewish children have lived for centuries without a temple (church). In many places they did not even have a synagogue (school). The fact that the Jewish religion has all the same survived, is to a large extent thanks to the domestic liturgy within the family. One that is strong and beautiful.

Christian children live today in a similar diaspora. In order to be able to hold one's ground, it is not enough just to have a short prayer before or after a meal. That is also important, but there is a need for a domestic liturgy: a liturgy of the *domestic church*, which is the family.

This domestic liturgy consists of the same ingredients as the liturgy of the universal Church, but in miniature. She lives on stories and symbols. She knows the same rites and observes the same calendar of the Church year. There is silence, there is prayer, and the family table is central.

Stories

The domestic liturgy has stories as its first component. They come from the Bible and are read during the liturgical year: from Christ's birth until his second coming.

In December, one reads about Israel and how it waited patiently for a long time for the coming of the Savior. All the characters of Advent pass in procession: Isaiah, John the Baptist, Elizabeth and Zacharias, Mary and Joseph. At Christmas, the child lies in the manger, and the shepherds and the Wise men visit. The period of Lent, means travelling with Jesus to Jerusalem, right up until Good Friday and Easter, the cross and the resurrection. From Easter to Pentecost is a time of uninterrupted joy. Everything is white and gold. And after Pentecost there is a green time: a breathing space, with the prospect of everything beginning once again.

The family – the *domestic church* – that reads the stories from the Bible, does what the Old Covenant required: "Tell it to your sons and your daughters." In this way, a communal Jewish-Christian memory, spanning a thousand years, was formed and passed on.

Something to look at

But the stories also need a visual framework: in order to put them into context and especially to make them stick. In a family liturgy there should also be something to look at, on the mantelpiece (if there still is one!) or on a cupboard or just on the table. There is the advent wreath in the living room, the Nativity scene in December, and Easter Eggs on the table. And in one place or another, a prayer book for the family or a prayer card. There are also icons and

pictures, and postcards from a sacred place that was visited during the vacation.

Ideally there is a prayer corner. This is in fact the most important symbol. A corner of the living room, or a place on the cupboard that has been set apart: with an icon, a picture or a small statue, the children's Bible, a candle and a flower. This is the centre of the sanctuary of a *domestic church.*

There are also other important symbols and rites that belong to the liturgy of the home: making the sign of the cross (the blessing) on a child's forehead when the child lies down to go to sleep (including the kiss) and the little presents that are good to have at hand: a mini-rosary, a scene in bronze or ceramic with a Bible quotation, a medal of Mary or of the patron saint, a little jewel worn around the neck or on the finger, something religious. Why only, again and again, the signs of the zodiac?

Furthermore, one should not think that what decorates the walls makes no difference. There are walls that glare at you aggressively and that make you aggressive in yourself. Or walls that challenge you. But there are also walls that you consider with pleasure, surroundings in which you enjoy living, that impart peace and security. There are interiors that "heal," and there are others that wound. In the context of Christian interior house culture, much is still to be learned.

The Liturgy of the Universal Church

The domestic liturgy obviously also needs the universal liturgy in the church building. Here and there, a good parish liturgy is to be found. Elsewhere, it is often below standard. There are many reasons for this, from impotence to laziness. The universal liturgy has a much deeper influence on children than people sometimes think. It is not always necessary to organize a special "children's

service." There are also the benefits of the larger church, of many people together, of the sacredness of the space, the communal singing and the silence.

True sacredness does not scare children away: it is more likely to attract them. Priests who celebrate with reverence and simplicity, spontaneously draw the attention of children to themselves. Being an altar server for the universal liturgy often makes children very happy and deeply religious, if they are well instructed. Too many children are allowed to "*stand idle in the market place*" (see Mt 20:3). They belong, however, close to the altar or in a children's choir.

Children often understand more of the universal liturgy than people assume. Auxiliary services for children are good, but they do not need to use infantile language. And moreover: is too much importance not being attached to the spoken word, to the homily? The silent and sacred beauty, the serene atmosphere, the reverend way of dealing with things – bread and wine – etch themselves much more deeply in the emotional world of the child than the spoken word.

The Table

It is interesting to observe that nowadays the family table is still in some sense the symbol of hospitality, intimacy and humanity, but has almost completely lost its religious dimension. For the Jewish people, this has been preserved. Sitting together around the table is for them always a religious experience. The priesthood of the father of the house – and the role of the mother who gives light – is beautifully expressed in this context.

The father of the house calls the family community together – as a priest would do – and receives it hospitably in God's name. That, incidentally, is the significance of the prayer before the

meal: it is the opening of a holy meal and the thanksgiving for food and drink and for all of life, exactly as a priest does in the offertory prayers and even more profoundly in the Eucharistic prayer: offering, praising, thanksgiving, taking and sharing.

This reference to the Eucharist is to be found in every family meal: there is one who presides, there is community and prayer – sometimes a short text as a reading – and the sharing of the food. Every family meal is like the *agape* – the love feast – of the first centuries and the reference to the Eucharistic meal. This *agape* continues to exist: the family meal is its successor.

This Eucharistic significance of the family meal in the *domestic church* can, and should, be perceptible in the way in which the food is eaten: with respect for food and drink, without waste, in unity with the table companions, in a serene manner and with profound joy at the shared conversation, with thanksgiving and sobriety, for one also thinks of those who have nothing to eat.

Gratitude and Wonder

Whoever gives careful consideration to the liturgy perceives that it cultivates two fundamental attitudes in particular: deep gratitude and great wonder. These attitudes far surpass supplications, lamentations and intercessions.

The *domestic church* needs to cultivate and deepen these two attitudes. The family needs to work at its attitude of gratitude and wonder. In this way the child enters little by little into the deepest understanding of the Christian liturgy. The child then not only becomes more religious, but also more human. For wonder and gratitude belong to the profound nature of humankind. And they are also the true initiation into religious existence.

Cultivating thankfulness presents more difficulty nowadays than in previous times: children today are used to a life charac-

terized by quick and self-service. They do not realize how much generosity is asked of nature and how much work has been involved to put bread on the table and meat on the plate. *Fast food* does not encourage gratitude. The family is in a position to teach the child about the long road from sowing grain to eating bread and to be thankful to God and man in that light.

Forgiveness

The Church is a house of forgiveness, because she is a house of love. And what is the highest level of loving if not compassion and forgiveness? This is also true in the miniature church of the family.

The atmosphere in a Christian family is one of mutual understanding and reciprocal forgiveness.

> An essential and permanent part of the Christian family's sanctifying role consists in accepting the call to conversion that the Gospel addresses to all Christians, who do not always remain faithful to the "newness" of the Baptism that constitutes them "saints." The Christian family too is sometimes unfaithful to the law of baptismal grace and holiness proclaimed anew in the sacrament of marriage. (FC 58)

This is why repentance, voluntary apologies and reciprocal forgiveness are an essential part of the mandate and the grace of the *domestic church.* Husband and wife and children discover how sin is not only at odds with the Covenant between God and humankind, but also at odds with the "covenant" between marriage partners and with the children. The family is after all a part of the Kingdom of the God who is rich in compassion.

The *domestic church* always spreads the fragrance of the perfume of the repentant woman in the Gospel, who anointed Jesus' head with nard.

Service to Humanity

If the Church is a house of service to humanity, then this is also true for the *domestic church*. Just as the larger Church, the family is called to the "service" of love for Christ and for the brethren.

Through a ministry of service, the family shares in the royal worthiness of Christ. The Christian family – just as every Christian – shares in the Messianic Kingship by sharing in Christ's attitude of service to humanity.

> Inspired and sustained by the new commandment of love, the Christian family – the domestic church – welcomes, respects and serves every human being, considering each one in his or her dignity as a person and as a child of God. It should be so especially between husband and wife and within the family, through a daily effort to promote a truly personal community, initiated and fostered by an inner communion of love. This way of life should then be extended to the wider circle of the ecclesial community of which the Christian family is a part. Thanks to love within the family, the Church can and ought to take on a more homelike or family dimension, developing a more human and fraternal style of relationships (FC 64)

A direct consequence of this mandate of the Christian family is the task of forming new people in love and of teaching them to practice love in all their relationships with others, so that the family does not withdraw into itself, but remains open to the community. (FC 64)

Is it not possible that in our time, this openness to the outside world, which expresses itself in hospitality, could be the clearest reference the family can make to God? Is it not He, who "in hospitality," takes us up into himself, re-creates us through baptism, feeds us with the Eucharist, and restores us through reconciliation? In our time of *cocooning*, hospitality is perhaps the most attractive form of loving and the most expressive fundamen-

tal characteristic of the Church: the larger church *and* the church in miniature.

Living Marriage and "Doing" the Trinity

Gisbert Greshake

My contact with INTAMS (International Academy for Marital Spirituality) coincided rather exactly with the period when I completed an extensive study of the triune God.[1] It was thus not by chance that my reflections on the spirituality of marriage were joined wholly automatically to the very heart of the Christian faith, namely, the confession of the triune God. Since that time, this link has continued. In what follows, I wish to develop this in a brief sketch. We must begin by going back a little.

God is Communio

Christians believe in the triune God. This means that God is not a solitary Person enthroned in infinite exaltation, no monarchical super-father, no personality who circles around in his own self. Instead of this, the God in whom we believe is community, an exchange of life and of love, *communio.* Since we are created in the image of this "communitarian God," we human beings are called to share in his life one day for ever. It is possible to misunderstand completely the statement that "God is community," if one were to take "community" to mean three autonomous, self-contained Persons who come together, to so to speak, to form a kind of "com-

munity of gods." This, of course, is not what is meant. Here, we must not project our human experience onto God. *In the case of us human beings,* community comes into being when persons who hitherto were autonomous take up reciprocal relationships, while always remaining autonomous in the exercise of their community. In God, however, there are not Three who enter into relationship out of a preceding selfhood. Rather, God's unity is an original relationship of love that lies beyond all our understanding, a relationship in which the three Persons communicate the one divine life to each other. It is only thus that the peak statement of the New Testament, "God is love" (1 Jn 4:16), becomes comprehensible: the three Persons in God are, so to speak, the "nodal points" between which the rhythm of love takes place, giving, receiving, and giving back. All three Persons are thus "one and the same love in three modes of being, which are indispensable in order that love can exist in God – and can be the highest and most selfless love."[2] In this way, the one God is the one interplay of love that takes place between the three Persons: loving, being loved, and loving jointly. And in this exchange of love and of life, the three Persons show both that they are distinct and that they are supremely one. The name *communio* is often given today to such a form of unity.

This is because this Latin word, unlike the *static* concept of "community," designates an *event,* that is to say, the *process* in which individuals find unity precisely *in* their specific otherness, by giving each other a share in their specificity and in their otherness. *Communio* thus means a unity that does not have its opposite, namely, plurality and variety, outside itself, but that bears these in itself. This unity means the communication among "many" who remain different. It is thus the communication both of identity and of difference: of a differentness that aims at unity, and of a unity that is realized precisely in the interplay of the many. Although a *communio* of this kind is known

to us incipiently thanks to interpersonal relationships, its deepest essence comes into view in the "communitarian God" who is the archetype of all *communio.* He shows us with perfect clarity that there is no antithesis between "being in oneself" and "being together." Nor do these two stand in an inverse relationship to each other, as one might spontaneously suppose: "The more I am myself, the less am I dependent on other and orientated to others; and the more I am dependent on relationships, the less am I myself!" On the contrary, we see, when we look at the triune God, that these two are directly proportional: the Persons in God are themselves by being wholly in relationship to one another and thus inseparably constituting one deity. Accordingly, they do not stand on their own over against one another. They are what they are only in coming from one another, in being with one another, and in being orientated to one another. The triune God thus shows us that the highest form of unity is that which takes place in the reciprocal relationships, and that the most fruitful differentness is that which is realized in the *one* common interplay.

We human beings are created in the image of this "communial" God, so that we may one day share for ever in "playing" in his life. It follows that we can attain this goal only if we ourselves are likewise "communial," for otherwise, we would be foreign bodies in the life that we are promised. Since we have been created as God's image, we have a "communial structure" *a priori.* But everything that the human being is "ontologically," in term of his essence, must be taken hold of and realized by him or her in freedom. Otherwise, human existence would remain stuck in the dimension of material givenness and presence. It would never realize its own specific essence, namely, freedom, subjectivity, and authenticity. This is why we must live up to our vocation and realize in freedom what it means to be the image of God, thus becoming more similar to the communial God. This

takes place as we move through time and space, in the encounter with society and the zeitgeist; and that means a tough wrestling with awkward handicaps. This, then, is the task that we all face in life: to grow out of our own narcissism and isolation, out of our self-centeredness where everything revolves around our own self, so that we open ourselves to the other person with his specific otherness, entering into an exchange of life with him and thereby realizing the *communio* that is presented to us in the guiding image of the triune God.

The logic and the inner consistency of the so-called salvation history in the Old and New Testaments demonstrates in detail that this is in fact the task that we face in life. The testimony of scripture culminates in the so-called "testament of Jesus" (Jn 17:1f.), the ultimate will of Jesus that includes everything and is the main point of all that he says, does, and suffers: "All are to be one, as you, Father, are in me and I am in you: that is how they too are to be in us" (Jn 17:21). The *communio* in which the triune God exists is to find expression among Jesus' disciples too, and they in turn are sent out in order to lead the world out of its divisions and into their own community (with God and with one another). Unity is thus the ultimate goal of the whole of creation. One could indeed formulate it in even more pointed terms as the "communialization" or "trinitarianization" of the whole of reality. What God *is,* namely, *communio,* is the gift and the task that we receive. We live in order to realize this. These few references to the biblical material must suffice here, since we now choose another path in order to go more deeply into our theme.

Marriage as a "Trinitarian Sphere"

When Genesis 1:27 states that "God created the human being as his image; he created him as the image of God, he created them

as man and woman," this also entails the affirmation that the human person is the image of God precisely by being created, not as an isolated individual, but as orientated to the other. Man and woman form the primal community of humankind, in a marked differentness and, at the same time, in an unconditional orientation to each other – in formal terms, in difference and identity, in differentness and unity. As man and woman, the human person reflects the Trinitarian God. As such, the human person receives the commission to care for the creation and "to multiply and populate the earth" (Gen 1:28), that is to say, to extend his own primal community. The creation thus aims from the very beginning, not at isolated individuals, but at their *communio,* at the union of the created being that is determined by plurality.

In this light, the gender differentiation of man and woman, and the vocation to the community of marriage, which is a result of this differentiation, are the "most original" and deepest vocation of the human person to *communio,* and thereby to become like God. This vocation is literally inscribed "upon the very flesh" of the human person. The human person, as a sexual being, is entirely oriented to the other with body, soul, and spirit, and undeniably experiences this in his or her own self. This shows clearly that one cannot discover the meaning of one's own life and the goal of one's vocation if one remains on one's own and perseveres in an inward-looking attitude. Rather, one must open oneself to the other. *Every* human encounter asks me the following question: Have I come so far that I can allow the other to be himself *qua* other? Am I so free that I can grant space to the other alongside myself and in myself? Can we come together despite our otherness, or better: precisely *in* our otherness? But what applies to every encounter is radicalized in the community of marriage. First of all, "the other" here is not just any other, but precisely the sexually differentiated other, and that means someone who real-

izes precisely the same human existence, but in a fundamentally different manner, as a man *or* as a woman.[3] Secondly, the community of marriage is much more than a temporally limited "encounter" between two persons. Marriage means opening oneself to the other across the entire variety, breadth, depth, and length of one's life, and living unity with the other. In marriage, therefore, the otherness of the other is experienced right into the marrow of one's own life. At the same time, however, one experiences that one can discover, or realize ever anew, unity and community, *communio,* with the other. Marriage is thus the preferential sphere in which the "communialization" of reality, which Jesus asks from the Father at the end of his life, takes place. As Klaus Hemmerle puts it, the unity for which Jesus asks "is attained in its full measure only when we are one with each other. It is only when we live in such a way that ‚you' are my life in me and ‚I' am your life in you, only when Trinity takes place between us, that the meaning of Jesus' mission is fulfilled and the life of God has become the life of the world."[4]

Marriage corresponds in yet another way to the triune God, because it is of its very essence open to the child as a "third factor" within the community of marriage, and thus realizes in the most emphatic way the basic structure of the community, which is realized by the threefold rhythm that can be seen in the triune God too.[5] But we cannot speak of this in detail here. This is why, as Hans Urs von Balthasar observes, the family is "the most eloquent *imago trinitatis,* which has been established in creatures."[6] And where the "fruit," that is to say, the child, is lacking in a marriage, for whatever reason, the two partners must be concerned to open their "I-thou" relationship to another "third" (common friends, work, interests, commitments . . .) and to constitute themselves as "we" in relation to this "third." In this way, they will realize "Trinitarian *communio.*"

At any rate, marriage is thus the most original – because it is inscribed upon the innermost dimension of every human being, in his or her sexual nature – and the most radical summons to realize *communio* as the meaning of life. It is likewise the "sphere" in which the human being's vocation to realize his or her being as the image of God, must be achieved in the smallest and most concrete framework that can be imagined. Since, however, the marital *communio* is the nucleus and the initial spark of *every* kind of socialization, it points and indeed impels beyond itself towards the goal of the entire creation, namely the communialization and trinitarianization of the whole of reality.

We can say more: marriage, more intensively than every other form of community, also points beyond itself over the horizontal *communio* (between human beings) to the vertical *communio* with God. The philosopher Ulrich Hommes formulates the link between the horizontal and the vertical *communio* as follows: "Love seeks the other, and yet the other, precisely by giving himself wholly into the hands of love, points beyond himself. More is present to ‚I and thou,' that is to say, to the two who encounter one another in love, than only their own selves. That which allows them to love each other, that which grants them this love, that which they find in this love itself, is also present to them." For it is in this interpersonal relationship, and above all in the marital relationship, that an infinite openness is disclosed, an infinite thirst of the human being which is not quenched by any finite "thou," but points to that "wholly other thou" that in infinite love seeks community with us human beings and wants to draw us into its divine-Trinitarian *communio*. In this way, the marital "thou" becomes the immediate bridge to the "thou" of God.

This significance of marriage – as a "school of life" and as the most original place in which to live up to the vocation to become more like God – has become ever clearer to me against the back-

ground of my work on my monograph about the Trinity and also in contacts and dialogues with INTAMS. Indeed, this became so clear that I was obliged to ask myself as a celibate priest a question that I must still ask: In view of this immense significance of marriage, what are we to say about "celibacy in accordance with the Gospel"? It is at any rate clear that if the celibate is not to hide himself away in a sterile bachelor existence, thereby evading the task and the goal of his own life, namely, to become *communio*, he must decidedly (1) attempt to realize a life in common with others (this is why, originally, celibate ecclesial life was in general also a life in community with others) and (2) allow himself, come what may, to function as a leaven of unity and a point of crystallization of *communio* among human beings. In these two points, married life is a sign and a challenge for each one who lives in celibacy for the sake of the kingdom of God (just as, conversely, the celibate can be a sign and a challenge not to overlook or miss the "transition" from the human "thou" to the "wholly other ‚thou' of God").

"Understanding" the Trinitarian God "in Doing"

The following legend is told about Saint Augustine. While he was working on his extensive monograph about the Trinity, he went one day for a walk along the seashore, wracking his brains about how one could understand the affirmation about *one* God in *three* Persons. He came upon a child who was playing, and when Augustine asked what he was doing, the child replied that he was using a spoon to ladle the sea into a little sandpit. This made the Bishop of Hippo realize that it is impossible to comprehend God. God is far more immeasurable than the sea, and he cannot be grasped by the "little sandpit" of human understanding. This insight led Augustine to formulate a proposition that has become

classic: "If you understand it, it [that is, what you believe you have understood] is not God." Does this mean that it is impossible to understand the triune God? Certainly, we cannot do so with our understanding! But there is another mode of understanding, which is hinted at in the picture in our little legend. It is not possible to ladle the sea into a little sandpit and to take possession of it in this way, but one can jump into the sea and swim in it, thereby experiencing that it bears one, cleanses, flows around one, and refreshes one. In this "doing," one "understands" much more about the sea than when one unsuccessfully attempts to become its master.

The same is true of faith in the triune God. Instead of puzzling, we are invited to enter literally into God, to "leap in," and thus to experience that our life is borne, embraced, and fulfilled by him. Precisely because God is *communio,* he does not stand over against us as a solitary, absolutely exalted Person. Rather, as the ancient Trinitarian symbol of the triangle shows, he is, in a sense, a "room" that is opened through the three sides, a room to which we are granted admittance *a priori* and in which we are invited to "join in the play." "It is in him that we live and move and have our being" (Ac 17:28). If we respond in this way to our vocation to realize *communio* in God and like God, we arrive at another form of understanding the Trinity: understanding in doing! Learning by doing! This is the original form of understanding that, according to Martin Heidegger, is displayed in a sentence such as: "This craftsman *understands* his craft,"[7] since this sentence means: He is a match for his craft, it suits him, and he practices it well. This is also how one *understands* the triune God anew, when one corresponds more and more to the gift and the task of realizing *communio* – in other words, when one *does the Trinity.* And since, as we have shown, this takes place (or can take place) in a very original and intensive manner precisely in marriage, marriage is

also the most original and intensive form of living the Trinity and understanding the Trinity in life.

This is surely also the deepest foundation of marital spirituality, on which we in INTAMS must reflect, in its presuppositions and its consequences, and it is this that we have to try to realize in the conduct of each of our lives.

Notes

[1] See G. GRESHAKE: *Der dreieine Gott: Eine trinitarische Theologie,* 5th ed., Freiburg i. Br.: Herder, 2008 (1st ed. 1997). For a highly compressed version, see my *Hinführung zum Glauben an den drei-einen Gott*, 5th ed., Freiburg i. Br.: Herder, 2008 (1st ed. 1998).

[2] This is how Hans Urs von Balthasar puts it in his introduction to the translation of RICHARD OF ST VICTOR: *Die Dreieinigkeit*, trans. H.U.von Balthasar, Einsiedeln: Johannes, 1980, 20.

[3] This also demonstrates the deepest problems connected with a "homosexual culture" that has spread increasingly in the last decades. (I deliberately use the term "culture" instead of speaking of the homosexual life that is lived in individual instances.) This is because, in a homosexual "world," the partner can never be more than the "relatively other." This means that he never represents more than a diminished challenge to realize oneself in and through the other.

[4] K. HEMMERLE: *Leben aus der Einheit,* Freiburg i. Br.: Herder, 1995, 27.

[5] On this, see G. GRESHAKE: *Hinführung,* 33f.

[6] H.U. VON BALTHASAR: *Theologik,* v. 2, Einsiedeln: Johannes, 1985, 56.

[7] See M. HEIDEGGER: *Sein und Zeit,* 10th ed., Tübingen: Niemeyer, 1963, 143.

Loving One's Partner as God Loves God

Adrian Thatcher

In 1989, Rowan Williams, the former Archbishop of Canterbury, gave an address on the theology of sexual desire called "The Body's Grace."[1] In that short piece he wrote:

> The whole story of reason, incarnation, and our incorporation into the fellowship of Christ's body tells that God desires us, as if we were God, as if we were that unconditional response to God's giving that God's self makes in the life of the Trinity.[2] (311-2)

Almost everything Williams says reveals a profound spirituality. He writes densely, and demands concentration from his readers. I have observed the responses of several classes of students to "The Body's Grace." I have been struck by their journeys from bewilderment to enlightenment. Williams' contention, summed up in this quotation, is at the base of the Anglican Church's deepest insights into the sacrament of marriage. The rest of this paper is a further reflection on Williams' vision for sexual love.

First, to say that "God desires us" is to make the conscious choice of selecting the language of sexual desire, of *eròs,* and applying this to God. This is a clear reversal of the ancient association of desire with sin. While some Christians might still be unwilling to disconnect the two ideas, there are good grounds for

doing so. Take, for example, how desire is handled throughout the Song of Songs. The most direct reference to God's desire in the *Song* is found at 8:6:

> Stamp me as a seal upon your heart,
> sear me upon your arm,
> for love is as strong as death,
> passion as hard as the grave.
> Its sparks will spark a fire
> An all-consuming blaze.

But, one may ask, where exactly in this verse? The last syllable of the Hebrew word for "blaze" or "flame," – *yah*, is a shortened form of Israel's personal name for God, Yahweh. It is explained that "... the all-consuming flame is also the flame of Yah: *divinity is the measure of the intensity of eros*."[3]

God desires us. But Williams is alert, second, to the human detail that there is as much or more joy in being desired than in desiring. He weaves this detail into a description of the *raison d'être* of the whole Church of God. "The life of the Christian community has as its rationale – if not invariably its practical reality – the task of teaching us *to so order our relations that human beings may see themselves as desired, as the occasion of joy*."[4] This is a profound mission statement for the whole people of God. It has its roots in the experience of a couple who, in finding that they are attracted to one other, soon learn that much of the pleasure of desire lies in the experience of being desired, just as great pleasure lies in the giving of pleasure to the other. "My" desire for an other is intensified by the knowledge that s/he desires me. If "I" can be an "occasion of joy" for my partner, and s/he for me, the knowledge that I bring joy to him or her is what urges me on in my commitment, my devotion and my deepening love.

Third, Williams says "God desires us, *as if we were God.*" This too is a reversal of the more familiar theological identification of God's love with *sinners.* Is not God's love primarily for what is other than God, for the sinner, for fallen humanity? Let us let Richard of St. Victor (d.1173) answer that question for us. Richard utilised the human experience of loving and being loved for the task of thinking about the God who is pure Love. That was novel in 12th century Paris. Interpersonal human love is his way of thinking about the divine Trinity. Richard argued that God is supremely perfect, so that in the particular case of divine love, another divine Person is required who, unlike a human person, can perfectly love God in return and is an appropriate object for the divine Love. As Richard says

> . . . as long as anyone loves no one else as much as he loves himself, that private love which he has for himself shows clearly that he has not reached the supreme level of charity. But a divine person certainly would not have anyone to love as worthily as Himself if He did not have a person of equal worth. However a person who is not God would not be equal in worth to a divine person.[5]

Richard's argument is that only *God* could love God worthily. In the Communion of Persons which is God, each Person loves the others with full mutuality, full reciprocity, and full equality, coinhering together in the union of divine Love. This divine Love is not only self-giving and out-pouring, but mutually self-affirming and self-supporting. God loves *God.* But Richard believed that divine Love cannot be contained by God alone. God's love must flow, gush out, embrace everything that is other than God.

Amazingly, Richard understood that mutual love between human persons could become a complacent, self-absorbed "coupledom" or "couple-ism." Richard observes ". . . in mutual love that is very fervent there is nothing rarer, nothing more excellent, than

that you wish another to be equally loved by him whom you love supremely and by whom you are supremely loved".[6] The love of human couples for each other has to flow out from itself to embrace others, whether children, or in a hospitable home, or in the life work of each of the partners. A third Person, however, is needed to avoid the possible mutual absorption and complacency that could afflict the couple. Richard thought that, in God, the Person of the Spirit, "the Third," was the Person through whom the Father and the Son share their Love with all that is other than God. "Shared love," he said, "is properly said to exist when a third person is loved by two persons harmoniously and in community, and the affection of the two persons is fused into one affection by the flame of love for the third."[7]

Fourth, we may now begin to appreciate a little more why Williams says God loves us "as if we were that unconditional response to God's giving that God's self makes in the life of the Trinity." We are not God, but God loves us as if we were. That God shares God's own life with us in our relationships is a belief that makes a huge difference to the practical realities of marriage now. The connection between married love and Trinitarian love is firmly established by Pope John Paul II.[8] Divine life and married life are both a "communion of persons," a *communio personarum.* While this analogy can be probed ever more abstractly, it is helpful instead to apply it ever more concretely to real marriages.

Fifth, concrete applications might be suggested by seeing how the facts of difference, equality, mutuality and communion, fundamental to the divine life, might apply to married life as well. Men and women are *different*. Different theories abound about how they differ and how these can be reconciled. But there is difference in God because Three distinct Persons comprise God's life. In that life, difference does not degenerate into separation or conflict; it expresses communion.

Men and women are *equal* in dignity and worth. There is full *equality* in God. All views of God which allowed for gradation, or for one Person to be subordinate to an another, have been rightly dismissed as heresy. The Athanasian Creed expressly says "And in this Trinity, no one is before or after, greater or less than the other; but all three persons are in themselves, coeternal and co-equal." Millions of marriages have been, and still are, ruined by male domination, by an imbalance of power which, in the life of God, would be unthinkable. Married life needs God's life so that power is shared and not misused. God's life is communion, not subordination.

There is *mutuality* in the joint administration of the sacrament or marriage. Marriage is the only sacrament that does not, or rather did not, need to be administered by a priest. Indeed marriage is the only sacrament that cannot be performed unless a woman is present. A couple is validly married (assuming no impediment) when they make vows to each other in the present tense before witnesses. The priest pronounces them married, and blesses them, but the blessing is not what makes the marriage (as it is in East). The presence of the priest or minister at a wedding should not eclipse the ancient understanding that the couple minister the sacrament to each other.

The contemporary point of this detail lies in the couple being *co-ministers*. They are co-equal in their *mutual ministry*. They marry each other. Two simple points may be tellingly made about this. First the joint ministry of the couple is a fine basis for equal regard and full mutuality over every detail of the marriage. The couple are full and equal partners in the common enterprise. There is no suggestion that one loves while the other obeys. Secondly, everything they do for one another is a ministry, an "administering"' of their sacrament. In a sacramental marriage the mutuality

that makes God's life communion can belong to husband and wife as well.

Notes

[1] It is widely available. My references are to E.F. ROGERS, JR. (ed.): *Theology and Sexuality: Classic and Contemporary Readings,* Malden, MA – Oxford, UK: Blackwell, 2002, 309-321.

[2] Ibid. 311-312.

[3] R. KEARNEY: "The Shulammite's Song: Divine Eros, Ascending and Descending", in: V. BURRUS/C. KELLER (eds.): *Towards a Theology of Eros: Transfiguring Passion at the Limits of Discipline,* New York: Fordham University Press, 2006, 306-341, at 308; emphasis added.

[4] R. WILLIAMS, as quoted in E.F. ROGERS, JR. (ed.): *Theology and Sexuality*, 312; emphasis added.

[5] RICHARD OF ST. VICTOR: *The Twelve Patriarchs, The Mystical Ark, Book Three of the Trinity*, transl. G.A. Zinn, New York: Paulist Press, 1979, 375.

[6] Ibid. 384.

[7] Ibid. 392.

[8] E.g., JOHN PAUL II: *Familiaris consortio*, section 12 (Marriage and Communion between God and People), available online at http://www.vatican.va/holy_father/john_paul_ii/apost_exhortations/documents/hf_jp-ii_exh_19811122_familiaris-consortio_en.html; accessed 21.02.2013.

The Seriousness of Marriage

Thomas Knieps-Port le Roi

If one traces its etymology, *Ehe* (the German word for "marriage") is not about an event of romantic love, but about a serious matter. This noun is derived from the Old German *êwa,* which recalls both phonetically and substantially the Latin *aevum* ("eternity") and originally meant something like an "eternally valid law." It was impossible and undesirable to enter in a frivolous manner into the covenant for life that was made between the marriage partners and in the presence of God. For most of its history, this covenant has marked the entrance into a dignified and sacred state of life that, with its stable institutional framework, offered legal safety, possibilities for personal development, and a meaning for life. Today, however, in an age in which more than a third of all marriages break up and alternative forms of life are available, we may be disconcerted by the seriousness and the weighty meaning which Goethe invoked when he described marriage as the "beginning and the summit of all culture," and went on to say:

> It makes the brute gentle, and the most highly educated man has no better opportunity to demonstrate his gentleness. It must be indissoluble; for it brings so much happiness that all individual unhappiness must be counted as nothing all by comparison. And what does one mean by speaking of ‚unhappiness'? Impatience afflicts the human

> person from time to time, and then it pleases him to regard himself as unhappy. But let that moment pass, and one will congratulate oneself because something that has lasted so long still exists![1]

In what follows, I should like to reflect on this "seriousness of marriage." I take my starting point in a literary model that belongs to the "primary rock" of Western culture.

In his two epics, the *Iliad* and the *Odyssey,* the Greek poet Homer relates how the king of Ithaca is obliged against his will to leave his house and his court, and how he returns to his native land only after long years of battles and war and interminable wanderings. In the Western tradition, Odysseus, the hero of Greek mythology, is usually presented as the archetype of human existence. With his adventurous journeys, he not only represents the human urge to discovery and the enterprising spirit; one particular philosophical reading of the *Odyssey* has also interpreted his story as an illustration of the return of the human being to his origin. The continuous wandering designates the dispersal, the disintegration, and ultimately the decay of Being, which can be overcome only through the return to one's origin in the unity of the one and the true. In a psychologizing variant, the hero's homesickness can also be read as an expression of the human yearning for an original unity and completeness that have been lost. This in turn explains why the human person always hopes that he can fill his existential emptiness too, when he satisfies his earthly desires.

This way of looking at things has left its traces on the history of Christian theology and spirituality too. Mediaeval theologians such as Thomas Aquinas sometimes regard the creation of the world as an *egressus,* a "going forth" of the creature from God, that can achieve perfection only through *regressus,* the "return" to the origin. A Christianized version of the *Odyssey* played a dominant role in instruction in the faith for a long time: earthly exis-

tence was regarded as a laborious pilgrimage or even as a "valley of tears." Not least thanks to this idea, a broad undercurrent spread in Christianity that was incapable of a positive appreciation of material and transient goods, and hence also of the body and the bodiliness of the human person. But one finds even today in secular schools of thought the idea that the human person can find his fulfillment only when he transcends the narrowness of his human constitution and leaves this behind him. One example of this is the Romantic ideal of love, which is very much alive even today. The search for the one, unique, true partner, the corresponding feeling of happiness when one believes that one has found him or her, and the wish that this may last for ever – all this seems to confirm the yearning that is related in the myth, the human person's yearning to be completed through (re-)unification. At the same time, however, this view of love means that the human person must not in fact expect this happiness within the boundaries of his daily existence. Accordingly, the sociologist U. Beck sees in the late-modern concept of love a kind of "earthly religion" which, just like the traditional religions, offers a "key to escape from the cage of normality."[2] There are certainly indications that such attempts to break out of time and of daily existence represent an attempt by love to escape from the bodily constitution of the human being too. The sexual passion and bodily love that today's couples see as self-evident were not in any way foreign to Romanticism either; but our yearning for an abiding erotic attractiveness and lasting sexual pleasure is directed to a body (one's own and that of one's partner) that ought not, as far as possible, to be subject to the passing of time, and thus to the processes of change and decay in time. The implicit imputation, which also applies to the body, is that the happiness of love should last forever, just as it is now – and only provided that it remains so! This illusion receives further nourishment from a culture in which societal standards of

renewable beauty and an inexhaustible potential project the image of a timeless body, and new technologies give the impression that they could reinforce the desire for immortality in its fight against the process of ageing.

When we look more closely at the story of Odysseus, we see a completely different view of the relationship between a couple, of the experience of time, and of the way one deals with mortality. During his wanderings, Odysseus is stranded in the company of the nymph Calypso, and he is compelled to remain with her for a lengthy period. Although the goddess offers him the prospect of remaining with her and thereby becoming immortal, he resolves to return to his wife Penelope. He replies to her wooing:

> My lady goddess, do not be angry at what I am about to say. I too know well enough that my wise Penelope's looks and stature are insignificant compared with yours. For she is mortal, while you have immortality and unfading youth. Nevertheless, I long to reach my home and see the day of my return.[3]

Odysseus decides in favor of the aging and mortal Penelope, although she must inevitably lose in any comparison with the eternally young and unchangeable goddess Calypso. The American philosopher Martha Nussbaum has attempted in an essay to measure the immense field of tension in which Odysseus enters through his choice.[4] She asks what could move a person to choose the death of one's beloved partner rather than to decide in favor of the possibility of making the partner immortal. According to Nussbaum, Odysseus' choice can be understood only when one grasps what the second possible choice entails, namely, a life and a relationship of love that would no longer be "human" in the truest sense of that word.

At first sight, the "divine" love of an immortal couple may appear even more valuable and therefore more desirable, when one

compares it to the limited possibilities that are available to a relationship of love between mortals. In the divine sphere, the boundaries that are imposed on earthly love are transcended, and love's possibilities are intensified to an immense degree, since divine love does not envisage any diminishing intensity of the experience of love. On the contrary, it envisages an unending desire and the equally unending fulfillment of this desire. But Odysseus understands that this comparison goes off the rails. In all "transcending," in all crossing over the earthly boundaries, and in all the intensifying of the human possibilities, there inevitably comes the point at which we and our beloved ones would not "survive" the transformation and transposition into the other state. We would then have landed in another life. Our love would no longer be the love in which a man and a woman bind themselves to each other. Our body would no longer be the body that we know – with its desires and its needs, its tension and its relaxation, its capacity and its weaknesses, with its possibilities both for enjoyment and for renunciation.

Odysseus' choice contains more than the common insight that we cannot in fact imagine an immortal life, and that the human person is conceived in such a way that, when the choice has to be made, one prefers to accept the risk of an unsettled life rather than face the danger of getting bored in eternity. If Nussbaum is right, human existence receives its profile, its significance, and its dignity precisely from the limitations that are linked to the mortality of the body. The boundaries that this imposes on the human person can be relocated only when one accepts them and does not attempt to leap over them. It suffices here to take the sportsman as our example. The contest acquires its meaning, and ultimately also its attraction, precisely from the fact that those who measure their abilities against each belong to the same species and are therefore limited in the same way. A competition between a hare

and hedgehog is not only uninteresting, but also devoid of every trial of sporting strength. Athletic achievements exist only when one brings forth the best in the framework of one's bodily possibilities and thus struggles in a particularly successful way against the limitations imposed by nature, without however leaping over the boundary that separates the sprinter from the fictitious being who can move from one point to another without any effort in a split second. But just as the athlete continually tests the limit of his capability in the hope that he can relocate this limit, one ought in love to hate and to fear the death of one's beloved partner and to do everything that one can to prevent it – and yet, one must accept that mortal existence is the only real form of life for the person whom one loves.

Odysseus chooses the whole human "package" of a mortal life. In marriage, the married partners decide in favor of the death of their partner – but not because death would be valuable in itself, nor out of a morbid delight in suffering, nor even because death belongs to life as a matter of fact. They decide in favor of this out of "love of the life" that can develop in a lifelong partnership and yet receives its full content only from its end. In the Christian liturgy of marriage, they promise each other lasting fidelity, "in good times and in bad, in sickness and in health," and thus also fidelity to the vulnerable and mortal body "till death do us part." This is the real horizon from which marriage draws its seriousness. It is the seriousness of an "iron" weightiness that binds the relationship of love to the earth and yet simultaneously allows it to put forth branches that reach up into heaven.

Notes

[1] *Die Wahlverwandtschaften* [transl. In English as: *Elective Affinities*], I, 9.

[2] U. BECK: "Die irdische Religion der Liebe", in: ID. / E. BECK-GERNSHEIM: *Das ganz normale Chaos der Liebe*, Frankfurt a.M.: Suhrkamp, 1990, 222-266, at 231; English: U. BECK/ E. BECK-GERNSHEIM: *The normal chaos of love*, transl. M. Ritter, Repr., Cambridge: Polity press, 2004.

[3] 5.215-220. English translation by E.V. Rieu (HOMER: *The Odyssey,* transl. E.V. Rieu, London: Penguin, 1991, 76).

[4] M.C. NUSSBAUM: "Transcending Humanity", in: ID.: *Love's Knowledge: Essays on Philosophy and Literature*, Oxford: Oxford University Press, 1990, 365-391.

Love *and* Patience – Sacramental Fragments

Herwi Rikhof

A book title with the word "heart" in it invites a certain type of contribution: a more personal or perhaps better, a more overtly personal reflection than is customary in an academic piece. But in the parish as well as at the university I have had enough meetings and occasions that caused and cause me to reflect on marriage as sacrament. So, from my "heart" some sacramental fragments.

I'll start with a fragment about a recent novel by Ian McEwan, *On Chesil Beach*. In novels, and the same can be said of operas, one can find stories that not only do reflect the sensitivities of an era or a culture, or do even present some more or less general features of marriage, but that also embody insights that form the core of a view of marriage as sacrament, even if that perspective is not intended. The title of my contribution is a slightly altered quote from that novel: I have added the italics. That quote contains an important element in marriage as sacrament and it forms the focus of what follows. The next fragment is about some recent empirical data and about a crucial change in thinking about marriage that can be located in one of the central documents of Vatican II. Then I'll turn to a theme that can be found both in Scripture and the theological tradition: the link between marriage and church.

The fourth fragment is concerned with the recent renaissance of the theology of the Trinity and then the theme touched upon in the first fragments reappears.

On Chesil Beach is a novel about marriage, or rather about not-marriage, about a marriage that never was, but could have been, or even should have been. On the cover of my copy three terms from a review are added at the bottom of the picture of a lonely figure on a beach: wonderful ... exquisite ... devastating. The picture refers to the final part of the novel, but the three terms capture well the whole of the novel.

Ian McEwan tells in the five parts of this novel the story of the wedding night of Edward and Florence in some hotel at the Dorset coast in 1952. While the first, the third and the fifth part are concerned with the dramatic progress of the evening, the other two parts are mainly flashbacks: about their different background, their first meeting and their year of courtship.

The very first sentence contains already the element that determines the fateful progress of that evening. "They were young, educated and both virgins on this their wedding night, and they lived in a time when a conversation about sexual difficulties was plainly impossible." The final part of that sentence is decisive: the differences in fear and desire, the difficulty to express those differences, the taboo surrounding the sensitive sexual aspects of marriage, turn the first night into a disaster with life-long consequences. Florence remains single and Edward has several affairs, a failed marriage, lives alone in his parents cottage and can admit after years that he never has met anyone he loved so much as he has loved Florence.

The most moving part of the novel is the final part. And the final pages are really the reason why I choose this novel as a starting point for my contribution to this interdisciplinary book. In the final reflections of Edward with which the novel closes, there is

an element that seems to me important, when we think about marriage. "All she had needed was the certainty of his love and his reassurance that there was no hurry when a lifetime lay ahead of them. Love and patience – if only he had had them both at once – would surely have seen them both through". Love *and* patience. It is precisely the combination of love and patience that makes this final reflection such a profound and moving reflection and also the starting point for some further, more theological explorations.

Empirical data are not exactly part and parcel of systematic theological reflections; most of the time they are hidden behind concepts or ideas, historical developments or biblical analyses. But a theologian reflecting on marriage or a pastor dealing with marriage preparation is confronted with these data, even if only with the decrease in numbers. And, of course, the interdisciplinary approach at INTAMS (International Academy for Marital Spirituality), emphasizes even more the importance and relevancy of those data.

Some relatively new data, at least in the West, are related to developments in medical care. People become increasingly older. Consequently, couples can have and often do have a third period in their marriage. That is to say, after an initial period without children and a period with children, there is third period when the children have moved out and the couple is "on their own" again. Such a third period does not only entail that, on average, marriages can last longer, but requires also special attention to the relation between the couple and a cultivation of that relationship in the "in between" period, the period with children. If in that period all attention and all energy go to the children and hardly any to their own relationship, that third period can easily become a deception, for after some 20 years looking after others, they have become (more or less intimate) strangers. The occurrence of

"late" divorces, after the children have left home, shows that this possibility is only too real.

The theological and pastoral importance of those relatively new data becomes relevant, if one considers the developments in the theology of marriage from Trent (1545-1563) to Vatican II (1962-1965), or rather the shift in attention from marriage as aimed at producing and raising children to marriage as primarily about the relation of love between husband and wife. In the pastoral constitution *Gaudium et Spes* (GS) the primary interest and emphasis is clearly and squarely on the relationship between wife and husband: their mutual love and support is not a by product or something required for something else, but a value on its own. "Thus a man and a woman, who by their compact of conjugal love are no longer two, but one flesh (Mt 19: 6), render mutual help and service to each other through an intimate union of their persons and of their actions. Through this union they experience the meaning of their oneness and attain to it with growing perfection day by day". And this primary attention to the relationship between husband and wife receives depth and richness by comparing it with the relationship between Christ and the Church: Christ abides with the couple "so that just as He loved the Church and handed Himself over on her behalf, the spouses may love each other with perpetual fidelity through mutual self-bestowal." (*GS* 48) The official form bride and groom have to fill in before their wedding does not only contain questions about data of birth and baptism and so on, but also questions about their intentions and in that context a definition is given, in fact a quotation from the codex, that reflects the new and revolutionary (in the sense of "turned around") development of the Council: "The matrimonial covenant, by which a man and a woman establish between themselves a partnership of the whole of life and which is ordered by its nature to the good of the spouses and the procreation and

education of offspring, has been raised by Christ the Lord to the dignity of a sacrament between the baptized." (can. 1055, 1).

When I was asked to teach courses on church and sacraments and had to select one of the sacraments as an example, I choose a few times marriage, partly because it tied in with my pastoral practice and most of the students were also preparing for pastoral work, partly because it gave me the opportunity to explore further the insights I just mentioned, and partly because in Scripture and in the (theological) tradition Church and marriage are connected as they are used to explain each other. Paul's remarks in his letter to the Ephesians (5:22-33) about the relation between husband and wife that he understands as a reference to the relation between Christ and the Church has been influential in the history of theology and spirituality. For centuries this has been one of the texts read at the wedding mass. Paul uses the term *mysterion*, which is translated in the Vulgate with *sacramentum*.

Due to developments during the Second Vatican Council Paul's way of talking has received a new depth, precisely because in the dogmatic constitution on the Church, *Lumen Gentium* (LG), *sacramentum* is used as a kind of definition for the Church. Although the term did not figure in the earlier drafts of this constitution, in the final text – and that is after all the decisive, authoritative and magisterial text – it plays an important and crucial role. As mentioned, it is the term that functions as a kind of definition: "Since the Church is in Christ like a sacrament or as a sign and instrument both of a very closely knit union with God and of the unity of the whole human race, ... " (*LG* 1).

It captures the view of the Church as part of the history of salvation, the Church as mystery. And it was that view that in fact was the stimulating force behind those heated discussions and it is that view that is still a stimulating force but now in the continuing struggle to interpret and implement the Council.

When the term "sacrament" was introduced as a term for the Church, it met with some opposition, if only because the term was so closely connected with the seven sacraments and the suggestion of an eighth sacrament did not seem right. That, of course, was not the intention and theologians had already proposed terms like "root-sacrament" to avoid confusion. The Council adopted the cautious clause "like" (*veluti*) and added as an explanation "or as a sign and instrument" (*seu signum et instrumentum*) in order to avoid that confusion. But it became also clear how fruitful this qualification "sacrament" was, for it placed the seven sacraments right in the heart of the Church and made the Church in more than one sense the context for those sacraments. The Church is the institutional context in which the acts and words of the sacraments "count", but the Church is also – and from a theological point of view primarily so – the community which is build up by the sacraments of rather by the people who are sacraments and act sacramentally. Although all the sacraments are moments, they are also processes. Of course, a person is baptised at a certain moment, but as Paul reminds us in that profound meditation on baptism in his letter to the Romans, being baptised in the past implies some actions in the future. "Do you not know that all of us who have been into Christ Jesus were baptized into his death. We were buried therefore with him by baptism into death, so that as Christ was raised from the dead by the glory of the Father, we too might walk in newness of life." (Rom 6:3-4). A person might be baptised at the beginning of her or his life, whether that person is truly baptised is only clear at the end. Similar remarks can be made with regard to confirmation, ordination and marriage (and in a somewhat different way about the other two sacraments, sacrament of penance and sacrament of anointing of the sick). The sacraments as processes, the persons as living sacraments make the Church sign and instrument of an union with God.

Precisely as sign and instrument, the Church and each of the seven sacraments have a certain transparency in common. That is to say that they embody in different ways a reference to God Father, Son, and Holy Spirit and even show in different ways a presence of God Father, Son, and Holy Spirit. But since that reference and presence is not just a reference to God or a presence of God in general, but a reference to and a presence of God Father, Son, and Holy Spirit, the sacraments are coloured by this central element of our faith.

Part of the recent renaissance of the theology of the Trinity is that the so called attributes of God need rethinking. Within a proper Trinitarian understanding of God an attribute like "almighty" will be understood in an other way than within a general understanding of God, if only since "the almighty Father" is then understood with reference to the life, death and resurrection of the Son. Jesus' behaviour in the Garden of Olives when they come to arrest him and his remark to one of his followers who used the sword: "Put your sword back into its place. Forall who take the sword will perish by the sword. Do you think that I cannot appeal to my Father, and he will at once send me more than twelve legions of angels? But how then should the Scriptures be fulfilled, that it must be so?" (Mt 26:52-55; cf. Lk 22:51; cf. also Jn 18:36). These remarks do not only run counter to a more or less easy and self-evident military understanding of almightiness, they also point to an element that is often overlooked in the reflection on "almighty": patience.

Patience is not only an accidental feature limited to that episode, but is the *basso continuo* of the whole passion-story, even of whole story of Jesus. Jesus' way of acting as teacher, whether in his dealing with the small group of chosen disciples or in his dealing with people at large, is perhaps the best example of this profound patience. The dialogue between Jesus and Peter before

the washing of the feet (Jn 13:6-10) has many layers and patience is one of them, if only to explain the whole process of reactions. Moreover, when Jesus after the incident remarks that the disciples call him, rightly so, teacher and lord, he adds to this remark a short discourse about servants, not about disciples. It is always dangerous to argue from things not said, but John is a writer who writes carefully and purposefully. To mention two titles with such emphasis and then develop only one, should provoke questions. The answer might well be that the other title is explained in what has been done. And perhaps, too, that the teacher is such an obvious example. The point (or at least one the points) of the whole story is the example set by Jesus.

It is not surprising to see some of that patience reflected in the way the disciples deal with each other after Jesus' death and resurrection. When Thomas, the Twin, is not present when Jesus appears to his frightened disciples and Thomas expresses some doubt about that event, that is neither a reason for the other disciples to exclude him nor an argument for him to stay away. For when Jesus appears again eight days later, he is among the disciples and the mutual patience pays off: Thomas' confession of faith is the impressive finale of the story (or even of the whole gospel if one accepts Jn 20:31 as the original end). It is neither surprising to find patience mentioned among the fruits of the Spirit Paul mentions to the Galatians: love, joy, peace, patience, kindness, goodness, faithfulness, gentleness, self-control (Gal 5:22-23 cf. 2 Cor 6:6).

Love *and* patience: that combination Edward lacked. That combination, he discovered later, – but sadly too late – would have saved the marriage that never became one. Love *and* patience: that combination is, I would like to suggest, profoundly Christian. That combination belongs to marriage as sacrament, if only because it shows how God Father Son Spirit deals with us.

Anthropology of Marriage

Strangers in Communion: Reflecting on Christian Marriage

Enda McDonagh

The foundation of INTAMS (International Academy for Marital Spirituality) itself and its integration of so many diverse strangers into a community over the years are at once an example of the new community (*kaine koinonia*) which St Paul enunciated as the fruit of Christ's Resurrection, and an expanded model of the communion of husband and wife which the Epistle to the Ephesians envisaged as an expression of the unity of Christ and His Church. Theology always needs the personal note of experience especially when discussing such a personal matter as marriage. For those of us who have not had the experience of marriage itself, the friendship of our married friends enables us in a limited way to share some human and Christian insight into the life and sacrament. In this short essay I wish to take a slightly more distant approach to human relationships in general and through further reflection on friendship to the intimacy of marriage itself. However this should not suggest some simple linear progression as different relationships, friendships and marriages may emerge at different stages for different people.

The key to good human relationships is the move from the unknown to the known, from the stranger to friend, from the feared

to the loved. Again these are not straightforward, sustainable and permanent moves. For all kinds of inculpable as well as culpable reasons, from death and distance to jealousy and property they may break down. At their best and persistent they will have their tensions and estrangements and require some at least minor mediations and reconciliations. These will be or should be the mediations and reconciliations of growth. For a fuller grasp of the dynamics of these persisting relationships it is necessary to begin where all relationships begin, even that most intimate one of mother and child, with the encounter of two complete strangers.

In the Genesis account of creation the divine power distinguishes the first humans as man and woman derived from the same stock and given to one another in a bonding love. Their subsequent estrangement from each other (they saw that they were naked and covered themselves), and from God (from whom they hid themselves), and the climax of that human estrangement in the Cain and Abel story, expresses Israel's effort to account for the history of human estrangement from God and from one another in face of their faith in a loving Creator God. Our contemporary world and Church is riddled with estrangements, hostile divisions between individuals, parties and nations. Yet the starting point of this reflection is not on the hostility but on actual separation and difference between individuals which anticipates the development of either hostile or friendly relations but has the potential for either. In an earlier expression exploring this area I describe the other or stranger as both gift and threat with the potential to enrich or diminish. Indeed adopting the description ‚other' as well as "stranger" enables a more subtle analysis of one to one relationships.

A central feature of most human lives, perhaps of most living things, is fear of the unknown, For the sub-human certainly it is part of their strategy of survival. It may play a similar role in

the development of human beings but because they are educable in such rich and diverse ways they learn to circumvent the fear and to get to know the unknown. Yet this can be a slow and difficult process. However much progress is made, the bulk of the unknown remains unknowable to the individual human being and in cosmic terms to the human race as a whole. And that is case whether you exclude or include a divine creator. This may come as a shock to some worshippers of scientific knowledge and its apparently indefinite range. They ignore or do not understand the limited nature of the knowledge which science provides even of the wonders of the atom and the tulip, and above all of the human person in all its dimensions and relationships. Human persons in relationship are the primary concern here and little enough expertise is needed to remind us of how little we know of the self not to speak of the other (person).

As indicated earlier all human relationships begin between strangers, between spouses, between parents and children, between friends, between work colleagues and neighbors. Not only do relationships begin between strangers, they continue, if they continue at all, between strangers. Indeed, emerging strangeness is a condition of developing, healthy relationships. The more intimate the relationship is the more the mutual strangeness emerges to provide new bases for closer mutual understanding and deeper bonding. Of course such new strangeness has also its element of threat and where the persons in relationship have not the determination and the ability to transform the potential threat into mutual enrichment the relationship is at risk. Too many marriage break-ups seek explanation in the mantra: "This is not the person I married five, ten or even twenty years ago." Of course not. Effective pre-marriage education should have emphasized that prospect of change. Continuous marriage support during difficulty should make it clear that the partners change and continue to change in

ways that are potentially enriching but may prove on occasion seriously threatening. Without change and adaptation to it there is no growth and without growth there is only boredom or worse unto death. The ability to recognize and celebrate the fresh enriching strangeness in the other is the secret of all fulfilling relationships including marriage.

Meeting with the stranger or other person is often in practice a mixture of projection of the self, its characteristics and interests and genuine encounter with the other as other. Where projection dominates the self is basically self-enclosed and unable to recognize the other as truly strange, as irreducibly and unpossessably other. This irreducible otherness is essentially to true recognition, respect for and authentic response to the other. It is an acceptance that the other simply transcends the self and may never become its possession or some kind of extension of the self or simply used for self-benefit. For the philosopher Emmanuel Levinas this is the beginning of ethics which for him is also the beginning of philosophy (and theology). The self-transcendence and self-surrender involved in such serious encounter is for him provoked by the exterior reality of the other and in that sense anti-symmetric, of itself not demanding a return. Of course the self is also an other who provokes the stranger-other (the original self in our diagram) in similar fashion. That other may not respond to the provocation to such transcendence and so the relationship remains one-sided, permanently non-mutual. However in living encounters the self-transcendence operates both ways and provides the basis for development of unity in difference. Such unity in difference has many expressions and varying degrees between neighbors, friends, work-colleagues, acquaintances, chance encounters and even media presences.

However its potentially profoundest, closest and most lasting human expression is in marriage, where it might be more aptly

described as strangers in communion, one-flesh communion. The very one-flesh description with its deeper mind-spirit dimensions reveals and emphasises the reality of the communion. Yet that coming together in surrender is necessarily succeeded by separation into the distinct others which may both be transformed in part by the experience of such unity. The dynamics of union and separation not just in bodily union and separation but in the daily communal living in the home or at work follow the patterns of self-transcendence in surrender to the stranger becoming obviously more familiar as the couple grow together. Yet the fresh strangeness which such familiarity facilitates and which in turn enables deeper familiarity with one another's further resources renews and sustains the spirit of adventure which characterizes the best marriages. Of course this fresh strangeness may carry its edge of excitement as suggested above into damaging estrangement. The older resources have to merge with the new in overcoming the dangers and strengthening the communion.

The resources for renewal and development are not in the Christian vision of reality merely human. In the Judeo-Christian tradition the ultimate Other encountered in and through the human other is the Holy One of Israel, the transcendent Creator-God and Father of Jesus Christ. In that context marriage was always regarded as a holy state as the bonding of husband and wife reflected the faith bonding with God. In the Hebrew Scriptures the relation between God and Israel were depicted in marital terms (Hosea and others) The metaphor in the New Testament Letter to Ephesians for marriage is that of the loving union of Christ and his Church. In the light of all this the Church formally recognized marriage as a sacrament in the thirteenth century, as an effective sign of the presence and power of God. Self-transcendence to the human other in marriage mirrors and realizes faith in the ultimate

Transcendent, explicitly for the Christian and perhaps implicitly for others.

There is another stage in all this which has featured from time in the Christian tradition. The God of Jesus Christ and that of his followers is of course the Yahweh of Israel and the Abba, Father of Jesus himself. However the fuller reality of that God becomes apparent through Jesus and the subsequent reflections of his immediate followers. The doctrine of the Triune God, of Father, Son and Holy Spirit is steadily clarified in the early councils of the Church and expressly affirmed in its Creeds. It was related to human love relations by various early theologians, some of whom connected the doctrine more immediately to marriage. The distinction, indeed uniqueness and equality of the three divine persons and their internal loving relationships has been invoked as a model for human community in modern times by theologians like Jürgen Moltmann for example. That sense of community between unique and equal persons is more clearly characteristic of marriage which already has divine connections. The integration of the Christian couple into the divine Trinity and of the Trinity into the life and love of the couple confirms the depth, exclusivity, fidelity and fruitfulness of marriage. And that fruitfulness whether it issues in children or not is by divine power and model enriching the wider world of the whole human community.

The Beloved Remains the Other: A Meditation on Eros

Ulrich Dickmann

> *"The passionateness of love [...] is a relationship to that which withdraws itself forever"* (Emmanuel Levinas)

Married love is a complex phenomenon. Three forms of love have been distinguished since classical antiquity: *erôs, agapê,* and *philia,* erotic love, (selfless) love of one's neighbor, and the love between friends. The core of a Christian understanding of marriage, as the encyclical *Deus caritas est* of Pope Benedict XVI impressively attests, has come to include the insight that these three forms of love, in an articulation that varies according to individual biographies, determine the mutual relationship of a married couple and establish a dynamic triangle between them. This, however, was not always the case. Although married partnership certainly has an erotic dimension even from an anthropological perspective, precisely this element was distorted in the Christian tradition over millennia, and was suspected of being a lesser form in relation to love, as this was understood in Christian terms. There are many reasons for this, linked to the corresponding philosophical and theological preliminary decisions and to struggles to ward off unacceptable ideas. For example, the Jewish-Christian tradition

faced the challenge of strengthening the concepts of life that had been given a new foundation through faith in the God of Israel and in the God of Jesus Christ, while demarcating these against the concepts of other religions. Since sexuality and eroticism were frequently understood in these religions as direct paths to the divine, they came under a collective suspicion – not least, because their kernel placed a question mark against the ideals of rationality and the ascetic domination of instincts and of one's own self. Fertility cults and temple prostitution, the "sacred marriage" in which the ecstatic, intoxicating element of eros was celebrated as union with the divine – none of this is suited to a people of God in which the dignity and the identity of each individual is a gift from God, and in which the path to God leads via the double commandment of love of God and of one's neighbor.

Eros can, however, be rehabilitated, if it can be shown that it is not directed *against* the reason, but against nothing more and nothing less than an immodest reason that is no longer aware of its own boundaries. The Jewish-Christian tradition is itself based on the insight that God infinitely transcends all thinking and knowing and all the images that people have attempted to make of him. What if it was precisely in erotic love that a dimension shone forth that proclaimed that there is something that lies beyond human thinking and acting? Would not that be a dimension that allows us to be attentive to the God of whom one cannot make any image? And a spirituality of marriage could draw on this connection between eros and transcendence.

In this essay, I wish to present an interpretation of erotic love that looks precisely at its transcendent dynamic in a wholly original manner that is relevant to the spirituality of marriage. I take up ideas of the Jewish philosopher Emmanuel Levinas (1907-1995), who attempted to translate the wisdom of the First Testament and the Jewish Talmud into philosophical terms. His thinking circles

unceasingly around the "other" who ultimately evades all thinking and knowing – in other words, who remains transcendent. Levinas noted the philosophical significance of eros already in the 1930s and 1940s. He was united in an intimate love throughout his life to his wife Raissa, who died shortly before him.[1] The erotic encounter between man and woman is an exceptional situation in which the ego encounters a human being who is completely different from myself: he is, quite simply, the other. I shall now trace the principal idea in this linguistically dense philosophical analysis of eros.

All human actions are directed to something that is other. But everything that is other than me is already "for me," and hence is not genuinely different in relation to me. This is because ultimately, everything to which I am in relation is available to me. The things that I handle and use in my practical conduct are organized by me; I make them my own, and thus take from them *a priori* their foreignness, their otherness, in relation to me. This applies also to my thinking and knowing: whatever I think, whatever I seek to perceive and to know, I organize in my own categories of thinking and perception. It is only in this way that thinking and perceiving are possible: my understanding sheds its "light" on everything that I encounter, and it is only in this "light" that I can see it. This means that everything that is other has been made my own by me *a priori*. It does not remain "other." As something that is thought and known, it is organized by me in such a way that it has already lost its foreignness, its otherness, in relation to me.

This also applies to the other human being, insofar as I perceive him. He encounters me as one thing among others. I draw a distinction between him and other things and other human beings, by comparing him. But what am I comparing in this case? I assess him in view of specific characteristics that I can describe. He has specific qualities: his external appearance, his facial expressions

and gestures, the features of his character, the way in which he communicates with me, and so on. In this way, I get an idea of him. But no matter how detailed my picture of him may be, it can scarcely be said that this picture is the other. He conceals himself precisely behind the image that I make of him, a picture that can never do justice to him – not because it might perhaps not be exact enough, but because, in principle, it is *my* picture, the picture that I have made of him. It misses the core to which the picture relates, namely, the other himself. He himself remains hidden behind all his external characteristics, no matter how penetrating my eye may be. In his otherness, he fundamentally withdraws himself from my eye, which always applies my own categories and criteria to him. This is the philosophical reason for something that we experience in our daily dealings with the other: ultimately, we can never do justice to him, because he is different, and he does not correspond to our expectations of him. We will never know the other human being. And this applies to more than the psychological dimension. It is, of course, true that his individual characteristics distinguish the other human being both from me and from others, but no description of all these individual qualities depicts him. Irrespective of how much I endeavor to be empathetic, he remains, as himself, other. Indeed, he is *the other*! This means that the encounter between me and the other always includes the real possibility of failing to do justice to him, because I get him, as the other, wrong *a priori*.

This initial situation seems particularly tragic in the case of our relationship to persons whom we love with all our thoughts and energy. In erotic love, we are filled by the yearning to become one with the other, to coalesce with the other into a loving "we" in which we are absorbed together. It is a sobering idea, that I and the other whom I love cannot ultimately be integrated into a common "we" of this kind. And yet, erotic love draws our attention

precisely to the fact that the passionateness of love consists in its being a relationship in which *two* persons who are fundamentally different from each other are with each other. Here, I encounter an "other" who always remains foreign to me, although I know him and he may be very familiar to me. Erotic love establishes a relationship of radical difference. Indeed, it is itself entirely woven out of difference – out of the difference between the one who loves and the one who is loved. From a psychological and sociological perspective, of course, erotic love establishes common ground between two persons. But here we must look at a deeper level in what is going on: the core of erotic love does not only consist in the fact that the coalescing with the other always fails. In erotic love, the otherness of the other is not abolished, because this ineradicable otherness is in fact the presupposition for erotic love. The passionateness of love is caused by the circumstance that two persons are involved. It is based on the tension that the other is not another "I" like myself, but is completely different from me. He is different from all the objects that offer themselves to my grasp – for the fact that I can grasp them means that I have in principle already bridged the radical distance from them. The other, *qua* other, is abidingly withdrawn from any grasping on my part. At the same time, the other whom I passionately desire is the one by whom I am affected, against all my expectations.

As the meaning of the word itself indicates, passionateness (*le pathétique* in French) is a phenomenon in which I experience myself as passive. Unlike all the actions that I perform and in which (as explained above) I behave actively in relation to everything that is other, thereby depriving it of its otherness, the passion of erotic love is the relationship in which I undergo something: I am affected by the other, I am surrendered to the other without resistance. And yet, the other affects me discreetly. In erotic love, the other, who is always withdrawn from the grasp of my perceiv-

ing and knowing, is experienced as *mystery.* "Mystery" does not only refer to the fact that the other remains unknowable. A mystery is not pure negativity, the pure absence of *something.* As pure absence, the other would not be capable of kindling my desire. "Mystery" refers rather to a surplus of meaning: not pure nothing, but the fact that I am in relation to a *someone* who *is* not only objectively withdrawn from my knowing and perceiving, but who at every moment withdraws himself, as himself, from my wish to grasp him. Ever anew. Unceasingly. The other is not pure absence; rather, he becomes present in the mode of concealing himself as himself from me. Let us recall here the encounter with the beloved face of a human being. When the beloved other looks at us, we see more than his organs of sense, his eyes, in this act of looking at me: in his gaze that is directed to me, the other himself affects me. All at once, his face with its expressions, its skin, and its wrinkles becomes more than merely a face [*Gesicht*]. It becomes a countenance [*Antlitz*]. It proclaims a surplus that cannot be measured and cannot be known by the reason, and still less by the natural sciences. And it is precisely this appearance of the other on the hazy border between visibility and invisibility that constitutes the way in which the other, as mystery, reveals himself to the "I": he is sublime. The other shows himself in his sublimity with regard to my interests and my skills that want to classify him. He is more than his physical presence – and more than myself. When the other presents himself in this manner, it is clear that we are not originally involved here with a second freedom that must assert itself over against my freedom. The other does not threaten me. On the contrary, his act of looking at me is absolutely unprotected, weak, and surrendered to my goodwill – and yet, it is disarming, since it does not make me his captive. I am, in a sense, transfixed by the other, precisely because I cannot utilize the achievements of my consciousness to classify him in my categories. He resists

all that I can do. He appears as the other in my relationship to him, and yet he remains unknowable and incalculable.

"Love is strong as death." This is how the Song of Songs in the Bible (8:6) describes the inescapability with which I am affected by the beloved other and by love for him. This love assails me and transfixes me – indeed, it inflicts a deep wound on me. It is, in the truest sense of the word, groundless. It does not owe its existence to a decision by the will to love, a decision for which I could adduce reasons. I do not in fact love the other because of this or that quality, or for other reasons that I could perhaps find. Instead, I love him. Nothing can be added to this. I am so passive and powerless in this relationship that I cannot even present reasons for it. And yet, it is precisely in this passivity vis-à-vis the other that I am confirmed precisely as "I," since the other sets his sights on me! He summons me as the one who is thrown off course by this unfathomability of love. The other stirs me up, and I cannot withdraw, self-sufficient, into myself and shut myself up against him. It is not possible to defuse the otherness of the other. This interrupts my circling around my own self. Love is disturbance rather than harmony, but at the same time it is a *dismantling of the boundaries of the ego.* The relationship between the lover and the beloved is a relationship of transcendence that introduces an interstice in the middle of the world, in which I have already reached out beyond myself through the other, who is "not of this world." When I am affected by the beloved other, I am transposed into an incalculable movement that I cannot bring to a standstill in myself.

The movement in which the surplus between myself and the other is realized becomes clear in the situation in which I caress the beloved person: I feel his skin, its satiny smoothness and its pleasant warmth. But it is not possible to touch what I am in fact seeking when I tentatively caress him. I am not permitted to grasp

the other, but this untouchability is not a mere absence, a pure emptiness. Rather, I seek something more, although I cannot say what this is. The caress does not know what it seeks, and yet it seeks. This not-knowing is, in a sense, already ahead of itself. The caress thus enters into an unceasing and intensifying movement towards a future with which I cannot catch up, a future that is indefinable. The tender "hunger" intensifies, because it is fed on ever richer promises. The loving desire awaits a coming that will not take place. It is characterized by the collapse of the hope of coalescing. And, no matter how paradoxical it may sound, it is this that constitutes the bliss of the moment, precisely because the other will never be under my control.

Does not this interpretation of the erotic relationship underestimate the yearning to become one together? I believe that this is not the case, since the decisive element is the unsettling dynamic of erotic love that is generated precisely by the tension between the strong yearning for harmonious union with the other and the simultaneous failure of such a union. Eros presupposes that I and the other always remain separate. In this way, a transcendentally abiding otherness is manifested, which allows the other person to take the path trodden by God, who has always passed on ahead of my consciousness, just as God passes on ahead of Moses (see Ex 33:22f.). The beloved other is not God, but love for the other opens up a space that I myself cannot make. It is in this space that I become aware of God as the one who is beyond thought. God can enter my mind, thanks to the beloved other. The other is thus the one who frees me from my circling around myself, from my egotism, when he sets his sights on me. He proclaims a future that points out beyond my own finitude, he promises something that is infinitely greater than I myself am. In this sense, love is stronger than death. Precisely because the erotic dynamic does not come to a stop, I am kept in a position of openness towards the other. Be-

cause I cannot catch up with him, I become attentive to his summons, to his needs and claims – in short, I become aware that he concerns me, although I cannot escape prematurely into the contemplative peace of a blissful togetherness. This shows that erotic love itself drives us out beyond itself towards love as *agapê,* the love that is active for the other and that is aware of its total responsibility for him and for his well-being.

Notes

[1] On this, see E. LEVINAS: *Le temps et l'autre,* 3rd ed., Paris: Fata Morgana, 1989 (1st ed. 1948), 77-84; English: E. LEVINAS: *Time and the Other (and Additional Essays),* transl. R.A. Cohen, Pittsburgh, PA: Duquesne University Press, 1994. – See also U. DICKMANN: "Eros und Transzendenz: Levinas' Phänomenologie der erotischen Beziehung als Spur primordialer Spiritualität", in: ID./K. WAAIJMAN (eds.): *Beziehung*, Schwerte: Katholische Akademie Schwerte, 2008 (Felderkundungen Laienspiritualität; 1), 63-81.

Marriage, a Sacrament for the Road

Isabelle and Alain de Layre

For all of us, life follows the same pattern: birth, sexual relations, death. For the majority among us, marriage is to be found at the centre of this path, where the fulfilment of sexuality is realised. The Catholic Church has chosen to sanctify this realisation through a sacrament, which expresses that God is involved with us on our – not always easy – journey, but one that leads to experiencing an ultimate love relationship.

Commitment and Giving Oneself

The desire to live love in an authentic way, leads to the total giving of oneself in an irrevocable commitment. The importance of the given "yes," makes it possible to conquer the test of time. Without faithfulness, love is not possible. Much more than an emotion or a feeling, true love is a decision that is sustained by a definitive choice, one that implies the abandonment of all other possible loves, in order to consecrate oneself entirely to one other.

One is then eager to do anything to make it succeed, because it is for life. One accepts the other as he is, but also as he will become. The state of marriage is not static, and the commitment

of the marriage partners is not limited to the day of their wedding, but applies to all of their future.

a) One's head in a noose!

In committing oneself to do everything for the other's happiness, one renounces the search for one's own happiness alone. This renunciation, through the space that it creates, makes it possible for one to open up to the other and for a mutual enrichment through which a happiness may be attained far exceeding that which would be possible for two parallel lives, lived side by side, but without being truly united. This idea sometimes awakens fear. Some are hesitant to take the plunge. Here, one needs to trust in the power of love that is given and received, a love which transforms and makes it possible to achieve what seemed unrealistic, uncertain, even impossible.

b) Cultivating love

This commitment is cultivated, is nourished every day, through the insignificant happenings of life, which are in themselves opportunities for keeping the flame of love alive. This needs to be the first preoccupation of married couples: to keep distinctly alive the pleasure of living together, to always be full of wonder for one's spouse. The love of two beings is like a fragile plant that needs constant attention in order to remain in flower.

At the beginning of married life, there is often a desire for total union that, after a certain time, is confronted with its limitations. This is a juncture that is at the same time both difficult and essential. It is therefore necessary to accept the reality of the other, accept that she is not as one has dreamed, and to relinquish the hope of changing her according to one's wishes. He, who cannot let go of false hopes, runs the risk of living in bitterness and frustration.

c) Sustained by the sacrament

In the exchanging of vows, the commitment has been made by three parties: God and the married partners. The Divine presence will never fail, one needs to trust in Him and to allow him to share in life's events, thanking him for the good moments, asking for his help in the difficult ones, fostering one's relationship with the Saviour through all the practices of the life of faith that we will consider below.

d) An authentic faithfulness

The faithfulness of the couple is never a certainty ahead of time. The conditions of the professional life of each person, the often very long duration of the life shared together, the economic autonomy of the partners, the influence of the media that trivializes divorce and adultery, the evolution of contemporary mindsets and of the law, result in faithfulness becoming marginalised as a value. For this reason, it is important to find strength in our sacrament.

In marriage, the partners commit themselves to creating the conditions for a communal happiness. This involves having, throughout life, the concern for the blossoming of the other and for his salvation. A mere physical faithfulness is insufficient, and may in some cases be accompanied by an infidelity of affection that is contrary to the initial commitment. It is absolutely necessary to keep this pleasure of being together alive and to continue the many thoughtful gestures that every person can come up with: love is creative!

People often decide to get married in the throes of experiencing the first fires of love, but this decision needs to subsequently mature, with reflection, and be continued through an act of the will. We often think that there is no love if there is no intense excitement. One concludes that if one no longer feels anything, one

no longer loves. In reality, the ideal couple does not exist; the true couple is the one that progresses through joys and sorrows. The will takes the relay of emotion and finds strength in the sacrament, which truly is a sacrament for the road.

Be cautious for the desire for a total fusion in love. Each person retains her personality and his tastes, even if their evolution is profoundly affected by the fact of being together. It is important to be able to have time for one's self, time when one can be alone. It is the communal differences that give rise to the richness of life together.

Communication within the Couple

We are convinced that there can be no life as a couple if there is no communication. If one is not careful, a wall of silence can grow up between the two partners. This communication implies a listening attitude, a desire to express oneself, an atmosphere of trust on the part of both partners. But it would be wrong to think that one needs to say everything; a total giving never occurs between humans. Communication only makes it possible to push back the frontiers of an otherwise reserved area.

At the beginning of conjugal life, one does not know oneself very well, and knows one's partner even less. The first stage is this mutual discovery of one another. It is important that each partner views the other with a certain marvel and admiration so that the other feels him/herself to be valued. Each person has in this way the sense of growing through the relationship with the other and his self-confidence increases. This pattern continues throughout one's whole life, and cannot be exhausted.

The second is the voyage through life, driven by the powerful motor of love together. In the process of this journey, it is good to look back together at the road that has been taken, to admit that it

was worth the trouble and to encourage one another to continue. The couple can then reserve quality time together, resting in the One who is all Love and who has committed himself to us on this path of marriage. The shared joys are more profound than those experienced alone. The shared pain is less severe. Through communication, each person can speak the truth and know that he is accepted just as he is. Being loved just as one is, simply for who one is, creates an enormous capital of trust! One also discovers one's differences.

To have learned to communicate on a profound level is invaluable during times of great trials, the loss of a child, illness, unemployment... the masculine and feminine temperaments respond differently in these extreme situations and this may cause serious tensions. Those who have gained insight into how the other responds, and take this into account, find strength and comfort in their interaction.

Communication is an art that improves gradually as one practises it. There is a phase of apprenticeship where willpower and courage make overcoming the difficulties of getting started possible. This is the time when one often discovers the masculine and feminine traits, the one has difficulty expressing himself, the other does so with ease; the one flees from subjects on an personal level, while the other prefers to dwell on them ... With regular practice, conversation will come to have a great versatility in its subjects of discussion, which may vary from the most insignificant details to matters of more serious portent. Here also, love is creative, enriching and trusting.

Another advantage of conversation is to facilitate saying one is sorry. If a conflict has taken place, talking about it in God's presence leads to the diffusion of many a quarrel. And receiving and giving forgiveness is the cutting edge of love.

The day will come, sadly, when one of the spouses will pre-

cede the other into the presence of God. It is advisable that a couple envisage and prepare for this separation, not only materially, but also morally and spiritually, in order that this time not be a time of desolation.

Fruitfulness and Sexuality

The couple's sexuality has three dimensions: pleasure, the relationship and fruitfulness. Pleasure, the motor of the sexual relationship, is the desire that attracts us, sometimes violently, to one another. However, for the sexual drive to be appeased, unlike the satisfying of hunger or any other need, the willingness of the other is necessary. It is the exchange of thoughts between the two partners that creates the relationship and that becomes, in itself, communion. The intimacy of the heart precedes the intimacy of the body.

The couple is, before anything else, led to be fruitful. Put analogically, the couple's love flows over onto their surroundings and contributes to the multiplying of God's gifts. The spouses, without necessarily being aware of it, reflect God's love, in their children in the first place, but not only in this. It is the vocation of a couple who want to be open to the world around them and to radiate their love. In this way, a couple who are "sterile," may possess great fertility!

Fruitfulness is then an all-embracing phenomenon. The love evident in the spouses' relationship leads to their flourishing. In the alertness they have toward one another, the spouses reveal to each other who they are and develop in this way all their faculties and everything of which they are capable. They are then more able to respond to the plan that God has for them, not only as a couple, but in every aspect of their social and spiritual lives.

The physical union is fruitful, even if not fertile, the pleasure being also a source of growth. The couple's fruitfulness goes beyond procreation. It consists above all of the transmission of love. The "go forth and multiply" of Genesis does not only mean giving birth to children, but also multiplying and allowing all the gifts and blessings one has received to grow.

Cultivating chastity means preserving the spiritual growth that will keep the power of sexuality alive and active. This leads to the true Christian asceticism that does not consist in a renunciation, but in the search for an authentic life. Sexuality should not be demonised, for it is a good given by the hands of the Creator. Neither should it be deified, for then man becomes a slave of sex. It is a human reality of life, to be lived out positively, for the growth of the individual and of the couple.

Tenderness is an essential way of expressing one's love. Through its gentleness and delicacy it is one of the most accomplished attitudes of love and touches the heart. Tender gestures are especially valuable when a physical relationship is not possible, due for example to illness or old age.

Marriage, a Call to Holiness

As Father Caffarel, the founder of the *Équipes Notre Dame* wrote: "Christian marriage is not only a reciprocal gift between the man and the woman; the consecration of the couple in Christ is also a gift. From now on, in this couple who, in giving themselves, open themselves up to Him, Christ is present , and this is why the saint John Chrysostom calls marriage ‚the Church in miniature'. "

The characteristic expression of this small church is the prayer life of the couple. The conjugal prayer is the tribute of our love to his love and makes it possible to distance oneself from everyday life and to find again the only and unique wellspring of life. Al-

though the idea may seem difficult, one should not hesitate to try it out in the most simple and natural way possible.

Every couple discovers their own form of prayer: reciting, reading, spoken prayer, silence at one another's side, in itself the prayer of a couple. What is important is not the form, but the prayer as it is, with its heart, and of experiencing it together. It is not then a question of two independent, juxtaposed prayers. Each takes the prayer of the other into account, is attentive to what she is saying, enters into his prayer and expresses the echo of it that it arouses within. Then the Saviour will be present in this prayer, in order to teach us to love one another more. The conjugal prayer is to be understood in relation to the sacrament of marriage, of which it is the extension, the confirmation and the resource. Each individual's personal life of faith, nourished by prayer, through participation in mass and the sacramental life, will lead them to respond to it.

Conclusion

There are a thousand and one ways on living a marriage. Each person is unique and has been created according to the inspiration of the Holy Spirit. The person is involved in his/her entirety, in his corporal, affective, intellectual, and spiritual dimensions. Love is an indispensable ingredient for a human being's equilibrium, just as the act of eating or drinking is for the body. This double movement of love, giving and receiving, is as essential as breathing. Mutual love has an extraordinary power: many have been profoundly transformed by their marriage. In conclusion, we should not forget humour, so important for smoothing over the frequent idiosyncrasies and sharpness of character which can make communal life stormy. Let us reflect on the words of the last beatitude:

"Blessed are those who are able to laugh at themselves, they have not ceased having fun."

The Grace of Being Two: How Marriage Makes You More Like God

David Dawson Vásquez

Is Marriage Important for a Christian?

Roman Catholics have what seems to be an ambivalent estimation of the value of marriage. On the one hand, marriage has been often seen throughout the history of the Church as a kind of second class way of living the Christian life. Paul taught the Corinthians that marriage is fine for those who need it but that it would be better to remain single and singularly devoted to the following of Christ (1 Cor 7). Consecrated virginity has been continually upheld as the most excellent form of the Christian life. Nonetheless, it is marriage that is ultimately called a sacrament, not the monastic life. Marriage, according to the official terminology, is seen as one of the seven signs that communicate grace in a special way. It is a privileged way in which grace is bestowed upon the Christian and upon the Church. Married life is thus said to bring you closer to God by changing you from sinfulness to holiness, making you more like God. For the most part, however, those who have been named saints by the Church have been unmarried. How are these two perspectives on marriage to be understood? Is this a flaw in the Church's understanding or practice? As I reflect on married

life through years spent living it, I can see how these two sides can both say something about the way in which marriage is a graced reality. In fact, I would like to explore here how the perspective that gives little value to marriage can actually shed light on the way that marriage communicates grace, in other words, makes one more God-like.

Before illustrating this, an explanation must first be given regarding the technical terms above: grace and holiness. We have the unfortunate habit today of hearing these words as referring to some special, "holy" reality that does not concern ordinary life. From the perspective of the Christian tradition, this is an incorrect understanding. To be holy means specifically to become a better person, to be a better human being, to achieve our full potential. To be holy is to become more like God, which means to become a more loving person, a better member of society, someone who brings out the good in others. Grace is the divine gift that helps us achieve this goal. Thus, to say that marriage makes us holy is to say that it makes us better people. Sin, on the other hand, is that which makes us less human, less complete, less loving. Grace enhances life, sin denigrates it.

Marriage and the Cross: From Complementarity to Unity

Married life has shown me more and more that married love requires learning to see beyond the superficial qualities that initially excited me about my spouse. Instead, as my wife and I have grown, we have come to embrace the complexities of one another's individuality. Forging a good relationship requires over and over again that we forgo one-sided expectations in order to truly understand the other's motives and actions, allowing us as individuals, as well as our relationship, to grow in unexpected

ways. There is a continual movement from the initial superficiality of the relationship to a deeper knowledge of the other. This allows us to respond prudently to the varying situations that come our way, even though the process is painstaking, challenging, and at times even painful. It is a genuine experience of the cross in our lives.

This experience reveals just how difficult a relationship is and how it is only through God's grace that we can develop a loving relationship. It is easy to see that we humans have a difficult time getting along with one another. No human encounter is easy. Christians understand this reality as the result of sin. Christ's action in our lives heals this basic defect and allows us to love one another. It is the only way that we can develop a real relationship with another person.

Even though relationships are difficult, fortunately there are some people we find easier to get along with, people we can begin a relationship with. We enjoy their presence, enjoy their conversation; they make us feel better about ourselves; they are physically pleasing to us. This initial attraction is superficial, almost structural: some kinds of people "fit" us better than others, excite us more than others. What we experience is a basic complementarity with certain other persons. The kind of complementarity varies by person: some may enjoy persons who are like themselves, others those who are different, and some will enjoy persons with similarities in some areas and differences in others. For most, this attraction works along the lines patterned by gender – women are attracted to men and male-like behavior, men are attracted to women and female-like behavior – with other more specific types of attractions contained within this general pattern. There is a wide diversity across individuals and the specifics of attraction seem a mystery. However it is experienced, we can say that we are drawn to another human being through structures of comple-

mentarity. I experience that some types of people – and usually some specific person – complement me, complete me, enhancing my gifts and compensating for my weaknesses.

This complementarity is what keeps society going despite the difficulties of building and maintaining relationships. We can usually find someone who complements us enough that we can stand to be with them for a sufficiently long period that we can manage a household, raise a family, work together towards common goals. Strongly-defined gender roles help in this. If men are expected to behave in one way, women to behave in another way, and both to respect these conventions, then relationships can function by virtue of this superficiality alone. There is no need to get to know the particularities of the individual because we are satisfied by the general structure of their existence. This is indeed how most every relationship begins. At first we fall in love with the general structure of the other's personality and the personal and gender expectations that we have of them. At this point it is the perceived complementarity alone that is the basis for the relationship. I know that the other is good for me because of the categories she fits into in my expectations

While this is the beginning of a relationship, for a Christian it cannot be enough. Those who seek to live a Christian marriage cannot be content staying at arm's length from another. When two Christians commit themselves to each other in marriage, they are not striving for mere complementarity; they are seeking to truly love the other. While this is not an easy task, they trust that God's Spirit will work through them, opening them to his own transforming love.

Complementarity is very helpful at the beginning of a relationship, but must be surpassed if we are to get to know our partner. Gender complementarity is a good illustration of how this works. We are given general expectations of how people function as gen-

dered individuals. These role patterns can be very useful in the beginning of a marital relationship. The otherness of the spouse is tempered by these familiar ways of being. We are comforted that our spouse does male-like things or female-like things. As we begin setting up a household together, these deep-seated roles and expectations ease the strangeness of the new relationship, helping us to feel at home in a new physical and relational space. We are gratified and comforted by these familiar aspects.

This is not love in the Christian sense, however. This is only the tranquility that is found in familiarity. Here at the beginning we have not yet begun to know our partner. Love instead seeks to go beyond this stage. Engaging with my wife as a real partner in life means that all my predetermined roles and ways of being must be continually called into question. I cannot hide behind given roles or expectations in order to protect myself from being changed by the relationship. Nor can I hold my spouse to these. The daily misunderstandings, insults, and incompatibilities that come to the fore when trying to get to know my spouse bring me up against my own immaturity, my own inability to get along with another, my own lack of care for the other. This encourages me to give more of myself, to open myself to growing in virtue, to have the courage to risk becoming a better person for my spouse, in the humility to recognize my poverty in the light of her gifts, in the fortitude of accepting the bad times along with the good as stages in a loving relationship. In learning to love my spouse I am learning how to love: my old sinful self is being worn away by married life and what is allowed to emerge is a new Christ-like self that can be truly open and accepting of my spouse. As Paul says to the Galatians, "I have been crucified with Christ; and it is no longer I who live, but it is Christ who lives in me" (Gal 2:19-20). I continually realize that whatever good is brought about through my

marriage is due to the transformative powers of the Spirit working within me rather than due to my own designs.

Marriage and the Resurrection: From Exclusive to Inclusive Love

My marriage flourishes insofar as Christ lives in me and in my spouse. What we are learning together is how to be better lovers, in other words, how to better accept the other in his or her own individuality and in this acceptance to give one another the space and confidence to grow more fully into his or her own unique humanity. What began as complementarity becomes a love that transcends this. The success of Christian marriage lies in the overcoming of divisions; the better our marriage, the less I am male and she is female and the more we are both loving human beings. The sacramentality of our marriage depends upon our living the unity that comes in Christ. As Paul continues, "There is no longer Jew or Greek, there is no longer slave or free, there is no longer male and female; for all of you are one in Christ Jesus" (Gal 3:28). It is here that the sacrament of marriage can be seen to function: it enables the spouses to be transformed by grace and grow in the image of Christ. It does not produce good spouses, but good Christians and good human beings.

It is in this light, it seems to me, that we can understand Jesus' statement that there will be no marriage in the resurrection (Mt 22:30, Mk 12:25, Lk 20:35). The resurrection is the victory of love which embraces all forms of human love. Marriage is an experience of the completeness of love, a taste of what all will share in the resurrection. This love is human love become divine, not a particular "spousal" love. Even in the present life, married love shows this. As we grow in marriage, we become capable of loving and of establishing good, life-giving relationships in gen-

eral. As we grow in virtue, we learn to love others better. This love is no longer directed solely toward our spouse or children. Marriage trains us in how to be open to others and how to develop positive relationships with the other people that we meet.

Married life allows the presence of the Spirit in our lives to strip away all that which keeps us locked in ourselves and shut off to others. We participate in the cross to the degree that we learn to give ourselves without reserve, painfully risking opening ourselves in love to others. In reaching out in love to others we participate in the resurrection whenever we celebrate and cultivate goodness in others, in society, and in the material world. Married people do not become holy in a different way than anyone else. The virtues of marriage are central Christian virtues. Although marriage is not essential to achieving these virtues, it is special because the nature of married life invites the development of these virtues in a more apparent way than the single life does. This is consistent with the Church's seemingly ambivalent attitude highlighted in the introduction. Marriage is special but not central to Christian life.

It is my experience that this hits at the heart of the joy of marriage and can possibly be a "technique" to a successful marriage. I become a better husband by becoming a better human being, which makes me a better husband, a spiral that, despite human failings and weaknesses, has the divine successes and strengths given by grace to continue growing and improving. Marriage in this light is grounded in the freedom and infinite possibilities of the life of grace offered to all in Christ. Thus a good marriage is not the image of an outdated example of nineteenth and early twentieth century masculinity and femininity of the like often found in Valentine's Day cards. Further, to the degree that the Spirit of God leads us to be more virtuous, more loving, to develop our gifts and talents, and to become more fulfilled, the more

my wife and I grow in unity. To the degree that we allow and encourage one another to grow into our own (often unexpected) graced existence, the more our married life is enhanced. The better spouses we are, the better members of society we are. Our love for one another becomes the source of our love for others that we meet. Rather than being a private fortress protecting us from the world, marriage instead continually opens us to the world, allowing us to engage with others in ever more loving ways. In other words, the success and the goodness of any particular Christian marriage are measured against its capacity to allow those who participate in it to become better humans and better members of Church and society. In the age to come when all are transfigured by grace, then the married will be indistinguishable from the unmarried in the qualities of their relationships with others and their engagement in the life of love.

The Many Fruitfulnesses of Conjugal Love

Giulia Paola Di Nicola and Attilo Danese

We prescind here from the theme of procreative fruitfulness, which we take for granted with regard to the fines of matrimony and to the survival of society. We prefer to look at the broader concept of conjugal fruitfulness in the many fruits of love. From a methodological point of view, we shall interweave considerations linked to the human sciences with our own experience as a couple. We regard our matrimonial experience as the vocational path to which we feel called and to which we have responded joyfully in nearly thirty-seven years of conjugal life, years that have been enriched by the gift of two sons.

Love is Always Fruitful

In a personalistic culture, motherhood and fatherhood are co-essential to the person, even when they are not realized physiologically in the course of a life: we are all created in the image of God (cf. Gen 1:27-28) and are therefore endowed with his creative dynamism. This fruitfulness has its origin in the love that is received and given (amor, "I am loved," and therefore amo, "I love"). This fruitfulness implies awareness that we were not

"thrown" into the world (Sartre); rather, we have been thought of, we have been placed in a context, and we have been called to a love that, without any constraint, appeals to the obligation to gratitude, in the logic of the gift and of reciprocity.

This dynamism, which is kindled whenever we feel loved, is triggered in a particular way when we meet the person who awakens an exceptional and exhilarating feeling that is so great that it determines life itself. The change can be seen on the faces of those who are in love: as Saint Thomas said, love *pulchrificat* ("makes beautiful"). It triggers a particular capacity to give oneself, to defend one's own love from internal and external problems (a place to live, work, various phases of life, stress, oppositions . . .). The whole of life is once again at stake: the way of looking at the world changes, as do the meaning of work and ideological and religious convictions, while one's children too take on a different meaning – a relational meaning. Love heals the wounds of one's infancy, drives away fears and illusory temptations, and stabilizes the couple in the affective balance that avoids succumbing to the psychosomatic illnesses (frustration, depression, neurosis) that are so often induced by cold and competitive environments. The man and the woman who love one another have the power to construct a new human environment and thus to found society itself anew.

These effects have a universal validity, even independently of faith. They are long-lasting, provided that the two see love as the treasure that must be given priority over the other emotions. These effects demand a dynamism of continuous change and of fidelity, in accordance with the circumstances of life; they require responsibility and care. For love is dynamic and fragile, like a child that needs to be looked after.

Married people must be on their guard against the temptation to fuse in a way that annuls distance and turns out to be hollow.

The distance is marked by the body, by the interests, by the sensitivity, and also by the vocation of each one of the married partners. The otherness of the other must be respected, if one wants to avoid invading and subjugating another person, while saying that one loves him or her. One who loves learns to recognize the professional, artistic, and spiritual vocation of the other, and delights in promoting his or her talents. Otherwise, unity is tyranny, love is violence, and the children are nothing more than claims that the parents put forward. Love flees from both individualism and collectivism and forms a community that unites by attributing value to each individual person. This unity in the eyes of faith is possible because the one who unites the married partners and all the members of the family, the Mediator, is Christ himself.

The Spirit in the Body

It is typical of married people that they speak of each other with the body and become "one flesh." The body of the other is, as it were, the prolongation of one's own body (cf. Job 29:15, "I was the eyes for the blind, the feet for the lame"). The sexual relationship should be neither demonized nor divinized. Although it must be on its guard against the risk of egoism, because of the fragile and obscure side of the psyche, the sexual relationship has a spiritual significance in this physical union: the caress, the kiss, the union of the bodies alleviate suffering, regenerate hope, and it is as if they transmit to the other person the caress of God, even when he is not explicitly invoked.[1]

In the case of believers, the obligation to keep the quality of the relationship high is more urgent: "As for conjugal love, if the two married partners are saints, it is the friendship between saints; if only one of them is a saint, the anonymous love of neighbor, applied by this partner to the other, is the only stable factor in their

relationship. If neither of the two is a saint, the necessary conditions are lacking. Conjugal love gets exhausted and disappears, despite the sacrament."[2]

That which concerns sexual attraction and love-play is not a preamble to interpersonal relationships, a technique used to attain the erotic object. It is a constitutive element of communication, a learning of the skill of going out of oneself, waiting for consent, seeking unity through the language of the body. By losing themselves and finding themselves again, each one in the other, the married partners bear witness to the relational destiny of the body, to its dying and rising again in the otherness.

The rules that apply to every gift apply also to the communication of bodies. The value of the gift is not intrinsic, nor is it measured only by the intention of the one who makes it, but by how the other, to whom it is directed, perceives it and gives it back. Love can change into an invasion, where consent is withheld. It must be joined to a modesty that casts a veil over the mystery of a human being – a mystery that cannot be unveiled totally, and cannot be reduced to a body alone. It is an invitation to look further, to enter into harmony with the infinite treasure that this body contains. The offence to the body, the union without consent, and the "adultery of the heart" wound both the soul and the body.[3]

The other is the litmus paper that decides the effect of a specific gesture that is ambivalent in itself: a caress can be a scratch or an encompassing tenderness, an embrace can be a cage or a joyful communication of warmth, a kiss can be a bite or an excursion towards the soul of the other, and penetration can be an act of violence and the acceptance of something that has to be endured, unless all these reflect the humble request of hospitality and the gift. The reciprocity sets the seal on the effectiveness of loving behavior.

The other always remains beyond that which is accessible to

the embrace, to the kiss, and to the caress (understood as a free "walk" on the body-landscape, which is the prolongation of a face). Similarly, the embrace is a "surrounding" of the other in order to overcome the distance and to welcome the other with open arms. The kiss attempts to reach the other at the place where his intimate essence comes to the surface, where his body opens to articulate the words that reveal him (this is also one reason why the kiss is used as a metaphor by the female mystics in their relationship with Christ). This is an attempt, not to devour the other, but to drink his essence. In the various cultures, the kiss implies respect (like the kiss of the altar in the liturgy), communion, or wishing someone peace. In any case, it involves coming close to the other, emerging from one's own self, and getting to know the other more closely. The conjugal act too should be seen as reciprocal hospitality. It appears that the woman receives and is passive. But in reality, in consensual love, the one possesses the other and *vice versa,* in the specific modes of being welcomed and of welcoming, of encompassing and of being encompassed.[4]

Even when they attain the highest unity, the bodies cannot merge together. They remain two bodies with different rhythms of life and of death. Each one must learn how to make the gift of his own body, not only in the conjugal union, but in all the moments that mark everyday life until the death that violently tears the body away from the person, but also transforms the body into a fertile gift for the earth and gives it back in the biological cycle to other human beings and to the cosmos. Ultimately, the path of spousal unity is a learning of how to make the gift of body-soul that Jesus realized in the sacrifice of the cross out of love for his friends, and that he had realized even earlier in the Eucharist, which is precisely the sign of the love that gives his body for food. In the various forms of human love, this path will prosper if it aims

at optimizing the reciprocity and takes the form of an analogous reflection of the model to which Christians point in the Trinity.

A Fruitful Complicity

The man and the woman who love one another recreate the world. It is as if they were a generating centre of new life. Above all, intellectual work must not be oriented solely to self-realization, to prestige, to one's career. It demands silence, spending hours and hours in front of the computer and reading books. It demands that one delights in opening one's mind to new ideas and to the encounter with unknown authors, thus conquering fragments of knowledge. Intellectual fruitfulness is born of the constant dialogue between two voices, the masculine and the feminine, which seek to reach converging thoughts and to test these against the external world. When they do this, they are responsible for a new creation.

We have often recalled what Raïssa Maritain wrote about her encounter with Jacques: "After the lectures he accompanied me home ... The way was very long and our conversations were interminable ... Nothing existed outside what we had to say to one another: it was necessary to rethink together the entire universe, the meaning of life, human destiny, the justice and injustice in society. It was necessary to read the poets and contemporary novelists, to go to concerts of classical music, to visit picture galleries ... Time passed all too quickly, and we could not waste it on the banalities of life ... Another One had pre-ordained a sovereign harmony between us, despite such great differences of temperament and of origin."[5]

Some kinds of work bring less gratification in terms of creativity and human freedom. Nevertheless, every couple can bestow a meaning on the drudgery of work by living it in relation to their

own loved ones and to society as a whole. Sweat sometimes looks like a condemnation ("You will get your bread with the sweat of your brow"), but it contains a relational and eucharistic meaning: each one contributes an indispensable piece to the great mosaic of human labor and consumes himself until death in order to make the world more human and more habitable, to conform it to the ideal Eden that must be reconstructed. In this way, there comes about a kenosis of the man and of the woman who work: a descending movement that annihilates them in things, and an ascending movement through which reality is humanized. (In the same way, God becomes a human being so that the human being may become God.)[6]

The Fruitfulness of Suffering

One does not love truly if one is not willing to sacrifice something or indeed the totality of oneself for the other, without making this sacrifice weigh down heavily on the other, without expecting a recompense, and without assuming heroic airs – one does it, quite simply because one cannot behave otherwise. A married person may feel powerless in the face of evil, but he shares the destiny (this is the literal meaning of the word "consort") to the point of feeling in his own inner being the pain of the other. This harmony in suffering has the power to alleviate the suffering, widening the heart and opening fissures of hope.

Sometimes, it is disastrous and unforeseen events that shake the unity of the couple: a financial crash, an illness, a death ... It is not easy to appreciate what is negative, glimpsing in it a summons to interiority, perhaps an opportunity for a deepening of the relationship. It is at any rate an event that heralds new paths and more abundant fruits.

The suffering is often caused by voluntary or involuntary offences. Blessed Ildephonsus Schuster, abbot and later cardinal, recalled that even the Rule of Saint Benedict demands that the Lord's Prayer be recited at Compline, for the following reason: "*propter offendicula caritatis quae solent oriri*" ("because of the little offences against charity that are accustomed to arise"). It is all the more necessary for a married couple to remain faithful to the rule of forgiveness, for this forgiveness is indispensable if they are to surmount moments of indifference, conflict, or betrayal. Sometimes, it is necessary to think again about the motivations for the marriage. At other times, one must learn to love without feeling loved, getting beyond the frost that has already invaded the relationship. This is the specific "wretched fate" of married people, their "cross." They must decide whether to flee or to respond secretly to the call that this pain bears in itself. This choice decides not only what will happen to the marriage, but how life itself will go.

There are many married people who see an unexpected wisdom and a far-sighted hope coming to birth in their soul, thanks to forgiveness. Whether or not they are believers, at a certain point they observe that the situation has been unblocked, and that the attitude of watchful waiting has prepared an unhoped-for resurrection of love. The sufferings they have endured then seem to bring an embellishment, with a splendor that can be perceived only post factum. It is like a tapestry that they look at from the other side, where they see the meaning of the whole picture. The pedagogy of love has made their gaze transparent and has prepared them for Love.

Notes

[1] See our book *Con o senza Dio? Per una spiritualità della relazione coniugale,* Rome: Città Nuova, 2006.

[2] S. WEIL: *La connaissance surnaturelle*, Paris: Gallimard, 1950, 76.

[3] See G.P. DI NICOLA: "Prostituzione e dignità della persona", in: *Prospettiva Persona* 27 (1999), 9-22.

[4] cf. X. LACROIX, *Il corpo di carne: La dimensione etica, estetica e spirituale dell'amore*, transl. G. Zaccherini, Bologna: EDB, 1997.

[5] R. MARITAIN: *I grandi amici,* Milan: Vita e Pensiero, 1956, 45-46. On the allusion to the "third" One and to his importance in the spiritual life of a couple, we refer to A. DANESE/G. P. DI NICOLA: *L'ospite discreto,* Cantalupa: Effatà, 1998; IDEM: *Amici a vita,* Rome: Città Nuova, 1997. On falling in love as an event *in statu nascendi* and an event of grace, see F. ALBERONI: *Innamoramento e amore,* Milan: Garzanti, 1979.

[6] See S. WEIL: *Cahiers II,* Paris: Plon, 1953, 190.

Paths to Maturity in Marriage

Crisis in a Couple – How Can one Salvage a Relationship?

Carlo Rocchetta

Becoming married partners is more than looking for the suitable person; it is being the suitable person, or becoming the suitable person. A large number of couples end up by separating without ever really having wanted to do so, for the simple reason that they have not found anyone who would help them, or because they have not found any way to read and interpret their own situation in a perspective of rebirth. Even if they may appear unforeseen, critical situations in fact hide a long series of episodes that have left their sediments in one or both of the partners. These episodes are marked by affective sufferings, mistakes, the inability to cope with elements of conflict, wounds, resentments, and rejections.

The Possibility that a Crisis in the Couple may Occur

Although conjugal life is *healed, strengthened,* and *sanctified* by the sacramental event of the wedding, it remains *a fragile experience,* since the nature of the man and the woman is fragile, as is their union and their commitment to becoming "one flesh."

The danger of a slackening that inflicts wounds on the marital relationship, casts doubt upon it, or even destroys it, is a threat that must not be underestimated. On the contrary, one must take precautions against it.

The possibility of a crisis concerns all couples, including those who are believers; no couple can declare itself exempt from this possibility. This is not an experience that only a few married people pass through. It is present – *potentially* – in every marriage, even the most successful.

70% of couples find themselves at some point confronted by a very delicate phase that has the power to awaken a crucial question in them: *shall we stay together or shall we part?* The American scholar Mira Kirshenbaum has published a book with the very well-chosen title *Too Good to Leave, too Bad to Stay.*[1]

There are *so many reasons that urge one to remain*: affection, the years spent together, being accustomed to life as a couple, the children, the house, safety, the awareness that one's *partner* knows one in an unparalleled manner, the fear that the future may be worse than the present. But *there are also so many motives that suggest closing the door behind one's back and leaving*: the intolerance of certain behavior on the part of one's partner – in daily life and/or in the intimate sphere – his silence, or else the discussions and the quarrels to which one is subjected every day, the lack of initiative or of creativity, losing one's way, no longer understanding one another, the decline of sexual desire, and so on. In view of all this, the couple is faced with *three alternative possibilities*:

First, settling down in the mediocre reality one experiences, in a *modus essendi* that accepts the humdrum of daily living, having lost all enthusiasm, going from one conflict to the next, with a great deal of unease, perhaps even pretending to oneself that time, by itself, will resolve everything. This *modus essendi* does not sat-

isfy anyone, and often results in a life led by separate persons in one and the same house, or in compensations of various kinds, including cheating and extramarital relationships (= *an anonymous, unrealized marriage*).

Secondly, fleeing from reality, breaking the conjugal relationship by separation and divorce, and then either accepting a life on one's own or else trying again with another person, in the conviction that one can experience with the new *partner* that which was not realized with the first partner (= *separation/second marriage*).

Thirdly, accepting the reality and re-choosing the person in a new way that is more mature and more conscious, learning to love him in his concrete identity (including his defects) and bringing to maturity *a new marital life* marked by the leaven of tenderness and by a renewed romanticism (= *re-choosing one another/falling in love anew*).[2]

It is obvious that only the third alternative leads to a successful marriage that makes both partners happy and creates the conditions in which the children can grow up healthily. Unfortunately, only a very small number of couples choose this third path, accepting help or finding someone who can offer them help.

The *crisis in a couple* should not be confused, at least in the formal sense, with a *quarrelsome couple.* The former refers to *unresolved* conflictual situations that tend to become ever deeper and permanent, and lead to the rejection of the other partner. The second concerns *occasional situations,* temporary situations of conflict, which do not lead the partners to put a question mark over against *being a couple* or against their intention to remain united. These situations concern at most *the behavior* of one or other partner.

This problem is largely connected to the way in which situations of conflict are lived. This can be *healthy* (constructive) or *unhealthy* (destructive); it may be only a case of occasional quar-

rels, but there may be profound sentiments of unease that finally shatter the very being of the couple in an explosion.[3]

The word "crisis" has a double meaning, the meaning in common use and the meaning derived from its etymology. *In the common usage,* this word is linked to the idea of destabilization, breakdown, or failure, which generally leads to separation or to the end of the marriage; *etymologically,* the term is derived from the Greek *krinô,* "to judge or evaluate," and indicates *per se* an attitude of confrontation and discernment in which one revises that which needs revision and finds an orientation to a new way of living and of loving one another in the marriage.

The crisis in a couple must be tackled from the perspective of this second meaning of the term, as *an opportunity to ask questions about one's own self with regard to things that are not functioning*. This is a precious opportunity. The crisis can then become *a salutary event,* since it allows the married couple to rediscover what is necessary if they are to become a "we," a community of life and of grace in the Lord.

Symptoms of Crisis

The problem is the temptation to close our eyes to the *signals* that reveal the crisis. These are *signs of health* for the couple, not signs of death. When a person suffers toothache, he is confronted by an experiential datum that causes him to suffer. But this is a salutary datum, since it says to him: *"You have to get yourself treated, because otherwise you will lose all your teeth!"* This is a signal that calls him to act to avoid a worse outcome, and to be healed. The same applies to the symptoms of the conjugal crisis. They represent *a message, a warning,* even if at the moment they seem painful, or one is tempted to ignore them. The symptoms must not be denied, rationalized away, or suppressed. They must

be confronted with realism and lucidity, since one otherwise risks noticing them only when it is too late. *What might such symptoms be?*

Loneliness

The first signal of the crisis in a couple is *loneliness*. This signal appears whenever the two no longer feel between themselves – entirely or in part – the sense of communion: a communion of hearts, of intended affectivity, of confidence and complicity. They feel that they are "solitary" rather than a couple.

Loneliness as the absence of dialogue. The most immediate form of loneliness occurs when the two partners do not speak to each other, or do so very seldom; when they do not find opportunities for being together; when they no longer spend quality time looking into each other's eyes and entering into a dialogue.

When they insist on the alibi of shortage of time, this is an indication that the married couple are experiencing this kind of loneliness:

> "We don't have the time."
>
> "It would be lovely, but we can't manage it, because there are so many things to be done."
>
> "We don't have a minute to sit down."

This is an alibi that conceals the absence of a deep desire to rediscover each other and to take stock of the situation. Ultimately, there is the temptation to flee from something that could cause suffering, and the obstinate refusal to look at what is not functioning well. One accepts the illusion that everything will work out in the course of time.

Loneliness as the feeling of being a stranger. The lack of communication reaches its peak when it leads one or both partners to feel *alien* and in fact *excluded* from the *partner's* world, from what he is and what he lives. This is an *affective* loneliness that becomes a source of suffering. To begin with, one is not always conscious of it, but it gradually becomes more noticeable and intolerable.

This kind of experience is a very dangerous signal of crisis. If no action is taken in good time, it can lead the marriage partners to live *like two "strangers" in the same house.* They live under the same roof and sleep in the same bed, but they do not live the conjugal "we" in a profound *emotion* that leads each one to feel that he is with the other and that he lives for the other.

The couple live close to each other, but they are like parallel lines that run alongside each other without a true meeting of hearts, of minds, and of life. The joy of constituting a community of life is sacrificed, to the profit of other interests, of personal hobbies or activities outside the home. It is not surprising if the two find no reason in the long term to continue living together, and decide to take divergent paths, with all that this means for their own selves and for the children who have been born in the meantime. It appears that between 60 and 70% of marital infidelities are linked to loneliness, especially when it becomes chronic and the couple do not seek help in good time.

Monotony

The second symptom of crisis is *monotony,* which occurs whenever conjugal life fossilizes into a humdrum daily life that never varies. The feeling of discovery and of novelty disappears. Marital existence is finally reduced to a flat and cold experience that is now devoid of either emotion or surprise.

Monotony as the absence of conjugal creativity. Monotony, either as effect or as cause, leads to the neutralizing of the *conjugal creativity* that allows the married partners to be renewed every day in the freshness of their love. One of the greatest dangers in marriage is settling down in boredom. In that case, the life of the couple is reduced to a mere repetition of gestures and accustomed behavior, and their married life is marked by apathy and immobility. This leads to the paralysis and the demise of the couple. And all of this is taken for granted – the appreciation of wonder and joy is lost.

Love needs to be kept alive in an awareness that never settles down into an equilibrium, and in forms that are constantly new or renewed. All this presupposes two basic conditions: first, that the married couple *do not allow themselves to be conquered by a culture that values only what is useful and functional,* a culture that reduces everything to an object; and secondly, that they know how to *give one another the marvel of being, the marvel of loving and of being loved, the marvel of adoring,* whereby they feel that they are borne by the heart of God as if eagles' wings.

"Conjugal creativity" thus signifies *a wonder that has become conscious* of what it means to be married "in the Lord," called to be a living irradiation and a mirror in history of the infinite loving tenderness of the God who is Trinity.

Monotony as a lack of "caresses." The category of "caress" refers to *every expression of affective exchange that is transformed into a message of recognition* of oneself and of one's married partner. The caress can be *verbal* or *non-verbal,* and it can take numerous forms. In whatever form it is realized, the caress is always a message that *makes people feel alive,* because it leads them to feel that they love and that they are loved. The American psychotherapist Virginia Satir has written: *"We need four hugs a day for survival. We need eight hugs a day for maintenance. We need twelve hugs*

a day for growth."[4] When the language of caresses is reduced to a minimum, or is in fact completely cancelled, this is a signal of danger, and this signal must be read with great attention. Married couples who experience a monotonous and tired life cannot pretend that nothing is wrong. Nor may they believe (as is often the case) that things will be resolved on their own, or by some kind of magic. Time does not resolve things: it makes them worse.

Monotony as an intimacy deprived of tenderness. It is not surprising – though this is no justification – that a married life like this leads one or other partner to seek outside the marriage that which both of them ought to find in conjugal life. When there is no longer any joy in being together, and the ability to wonder is lost, *sexuality itself is reduced to a mere material fact or only to the satisfaction of instincts.* It is a self-enclosed episode without any real experience of love. Only a tenderness that makes the partners feel loved and that is renewed from day to day is able to overcome the wear and tear of time and to bestow on conjugal intimacy the wonderful meaning of the encounter, of the ever new enchantment of an act of giving oneself and receiving oneself that is never something taken for granted or a weary repetition of gestures.

The State of Revenge

The most direct consequence of the signals we have mentioned is to engender in one or in both of the married partners *a state of revenge* that lies in wait, like fire under ashes, and can explode at any moment.

The "faces" of revenge. The state of revenge can take on many various forms. There is the "face" of the *internal tensions that acquire a bodily form* and are transformed into psycho-physical ill-

nesses or into repeated quarrels with verbal aggressions, forms of contempt and inner hardness, reactions of exasperation, and gratuitous violence. There is the "face" of *discontent,* which laments continually and keeps on making accusations; the partners are intolerant, are shut up in their own world, or look for affirmation of themselves through defence or attack, even at the cost of the higher good of the community of the partners and of their children. This discontent is manifested whenever one of the two tries to punish the other with words or acts that strike home (the so-called "intelligent missiles"), or with killing words that hurt the other as much as possible.

There is the "face" of *destructive conflictuality,* when the life of the couple is thought of as a duel in which one wins and the other loses, but where in reality both partners are the losers, because the one who has suffered will cultivate in himself thoughts of revenge that will explode when one least expects it. A "hellish" cycle will be actualized even on very petty occasions, becoming more and more severe and creating unease and divisions. The conjugal crisis must not be regarded as a boxing ring with a winner and a loser, but as a space of communication in which there are only winners. Finally, there is the "face" of the *rivalry* of one partner against the other, when instead of being happy and rejoicing at the success of the other, one suffers because of this, and feelings of hostility and of revenge arise. This is a signal that turns married life into an arena of *competition,* going as far as intolerance and rejection. The marriage becomes a contest in a continuous tension that makes the partners tired and breaks them down. There is no longer any joy or reciprocal satisfaction.

Revenge as "do ut des." The logic that prevails in all the circumstances mentioned above is calculating, and even blackmailing: *do ut des,* "I give if I receive, and only to the extent that I re-

ceive." Variants of the same logic are also found: *"What do* you *do for* me*?"*, *"I love you if you love me," "I will love you only when you ask me to forgive you."* Whatever form it takes, the calculating logic reduces married life to a cohabitation of accountants who think in terms of credit and debit. This is the very antithesis of marital love. When the partners realize that their existence is sliding down into this kind of outcome, they must attune their antennas well and undertake a very sincere and profound examination. The "vicious circle" is broken and becomes a "virtuous circle" only if each of the two stops locating himself on the level of the *do ut des,* and asks himself:

> "What am I doing for him/her, so that he/she may be happy?"
>
> "I love you even if you do not show love to me."
>
> "I ask for pardon, even if you do not do so."

The Lack of Spirituality

The lack of spirituality is no less important as a symptom of the conjugal crisis. By this, I mean indifference, coldness, or rejection of the values of transcendence and of faith. This attitude is empty of God. In the present reflections, we place this symptom last, but it is in reality the first symptom and the root of all the others, for it is not possible to have a mature and lasting realization of married life, if the partners do not educate themselves to *experience a profound communion in God who is Trinity, the God who has united them, who saves them, and who can give them new birth every day as "ministers of grace" for each other.*

"Hear, O Israel" (Dt 6:4). The fundamental norm of the chosen people applies to the couple: they must listen to God in order to be able to listen to one another. The acts of listening are inseparable: *the more the couples learn to listen to God, and do this*

together in a climate of truth and humility, the more they grow in listening to each other. If the couple do not educate themselves to become *good listeners to God,* it will be difficult for them to be *good listeners to each other,* and *vice versa.*

For Christian couples, this is not a question of choosing between God and one's married partner, but of *loving the One in loving the other, listening to the One in listening to the other.* The unity of the two loves and of the two acts of listening comes about through this profound interaction, and leads the couple to grow in a loving tenderness that is renewed from day to day, as a gift of grace that is always new.

In this perspective, faith plays a decisive role in overcoming the crisis of the couple, since believing in God means believing that there is no difficult situation that cannot be overcome. Faith means that one can benefit from an added value, in the awareness that the couple is not alone. In this way, they become willing to go along the path, no matter how long it may be.

Indifference with regard to faith. Unfortunately, most couples regard the encounter with God as of marginal importance for the realization of their marriage. In reality, however, it is only in the encounter with the Absolute of Love that the couple educate themselves to ask for pardon and to pardon, learning the art of *comprehension* ("understanding *with*"), *compassion* ("suffering *with*"), *responsibility,* and *fidelity,* along with the ability to overcome the wounds and the temptations to yield to distrust or discouragement.

Indifference with regard to faith may rightly be considered a lack, a gap that creates a boundary and does not allow the married couple to refine the spiritual sensitivity that alone is able to build up the communion of the couple and to realize the grace of the sacrament. Praying together (to take one example) leads the life of the couple back to the divine spring from which their being

and all their tenderness flow, and educates them to be authentic, capable of the true gift, true welcome, and true sharing.

Tenderness as the Antidote to the Crisis[5]

The profound reason for the conjugal crisis lies in the lack of tenderness that has arisen between the two partners. It is no exaggeration to affirm that a large number of conjugal pathologies derive from this lack, which causes the disappearance of a love that renews itself from day to day, as well as of the highest meaning of conjugal sexuality itself.

The antidote that brings healing consists in searching for *a marital tenderness capable of allowing the other partner to feel loved and appreciated.* This antidote demands, first of all, that the couple know how to cultivate quality time to talk to one another, to educate themselves in listening and in communicating, heart to heart; and secondly, that they learn to take care of one another, seeking to be attentive to each one's needs. When this is missing, it is inevitable that the couple will start to send out the signals mentioned above, and that they will feel a strong sense of frustration, marked by *anger, fear,* and *sadness.*

Tenderness is the exact opposite of these three feelings:

First, the couple who choose tenderness cannot be overwhelmed by the power of anger, because tenderness is, by definition, *a loving attitude, respect of oneself and of others, empathy, and sympathy.* One could call it a "new lightness of being."

Secondly, the couple who choose tenderness cannot have any room for fear or anxiety, because tenderness is *trust in what we are and in what we can become, trust in God and entrusting oneself to his providence,* giving thanks with one's life, feeling loved and loving.

Thirdly, the couple who choose tenderness cannot be dominated by sadness, because tenderness is joy and interior peace: *it is the bliss of being, of loving, of adoring.*

Choosing tenderness as a couple means an orientation towards transforming all the difficulties into opportunities for growth. These difficulties are now perceived, not in a destructive framework, but as the signal of a conversion and of a path that must be undertaken towards tenderness. The conjugal option for tenderness as a basic emotion begins when they stop blaming the other (*anger*) or their own selves (*fear/anxiety*) or both of them (*sadness*), and begin asking: *"What can I as a married partner do to make my partner happy?" and vice versa.*

The fundamental attitude is a refusal to shut oneself up within the precincts of one's own egotism. One chooses to *expose* oneself, one emerges from oneself in order to become a travelling companion and a friend of the other in an attitude of *gift,* of *welcome,* and of *sharing.*

Married people are called *to attend the school of tenderness,* overcoming the affective illiteracy that is so prevalent today and learning how to be mutually enriched by the gifts that they bear, in order to construct together a dialogue that respects their difference, a true "we," a family that is a "house of tenderness" and a first school of tenderness for their children.

What does it mean for the man and the woman to attend "the school of tenderness"? It certainly means *opening themselves to the ineffable horizons of the Absolute Tenderness, of the God who is Trinity.* Is not God the inexhaustible spring and the summit of all tenderness, for those who let themselves be loved by him and who learn, in him, to love tenderly life and even the smallest reality in creation? The married partners are called to grow to maturity in this awareness, feeling themselves to be in the very heart of the

Trinity, loved by the God who is Trinity and borne by him as if on eagles' wings.

The Lebanese poet Kahlil Gibran states this in these marvellous words: "When you love you should not say, 'God is in my heart,' but rather, 'I am in the heart of God.'"[6]

Conclusion

Tenderness has an inner propulsion towards being transformed into *"the power of humble love,"* which is a clear antithesis to *the brutality of force*. The Russian monk Zosima evokes this in a very beautiful passage in *The Brothers Karamazov*:[7]

> At some thoughts one stands perplexed, especially at the sight of men's sin, and wonders whether one should use force or humble love. Always decide to use humble love. If you resolve on that once for all, you may subdue the whole world. Loving humility is marvelously strong, the strongest of all things, and there is nothing else like it.

Notes

[1] M. KIRSCHENBAUM: *Too Good to Leave, too Bad to Stay: A Step-by-step Guide to Help You Decide whether to Stay in or Get out of Your Relationship*, New York: Wiley & Sons, 1996.

[2] On this third possibility, see C. ROCCHETTA: *Viaggio nella tenerezza nuziale: Per ri-innamorarsi ogni giorno,* 4th ed., Bologna: EDB, 2007.

[3] On this distinction, see my book *Elogio del litigio di coppia,* Bologna: EDB, 2004, 17-41.

[4] Reported in *Sojourners* (March 1981).

[5] I refer in this context to my book *Teologia della tenerezza: Un "Vangelo" da riscoprire*, 4th ed., Bologna: EDB, 2005. On the spirituality of the married couple in the perspective of tenderness, see C. ROCCHETTA: *Viaggio nella tenerezza nuziale*; IDEM: *Elogio del litigio di coppia*; IDEM: *Gesù medico*

degli sposi: La tenerezza che guarisce, Bologna: EDB, 2006; IDEM: *Le stagioni dell'amore: Fidanzati e sposi in cammino con il Cantico dei Cantici,* Bologna: EDB, 2006. On the theology of the sacrament of matrimony, see IDEM: *Il sacramento della coppia: Saggio di teologia del matrimonio cristiano,* 4th ed., Bologna: EDB, 2003.

[6] G.K. Gibran: *The Prophet,* New York: Knopf, 1995, 10.

[7] Ch. 41.

A Gift for Life

Ilse Cornu

Many relationships of love break down. And even for couples who love one another, love does not last forever. Indeed, love can turn into its opposite, so that people who have genuinely loved one another begin to destroy one another. Unrealistic and perverted ideals of love can also lead people to crucify each other. Or else, a lack of acceptance distorts the perception of the other and of one's own person. When one no longer encounters the other in openness, it becomes difficult to put up with the otherness of the person one loves.

Is love merely an empty word? Are true love and a happy marriage merely illusions? When we seek to focus on the sacrament of marriage, we cannot evade these questions. Nor can we evade the imperfection of love. This essay attempts to set out in various ways how married people can respect the vulnerability and the imperfection of the other person without losing their own selves, so that new life becomes possible.

Emptiness and Sobriety

The Apostle Paul locates marital love in the mystery of Christ: "For this reason a man will leave his father and mother and be

joined to his wife, and the two will become one flesh. This is a great mystery, and I am applying it to Christ and the church" (Eph 5:31). We can also understand this to mean that marital love has a share in the story of Christ's love and of his suffering. This refers, on the one hand, to Christ's desire to receive God's life-giving love and to hand it on, and on the other hand, to the path of suffering from which no form of human or divine love is exempt.

In his book *Le paradoxe infini,* the French priest and philosopher Maurice Bellet asks: "Que reste-t-il quand il ne reste rien?" ("What is left, when nothing is left?").[1] He attempts thereby a new formulation of Christ's words on the cross: "My God, my God, why have you forsaken me?" How is it possible for the life-giving love still to offer support, when a path through life becomes a path of suffering that apparently ends in failure and death? According to Maurice Bellet, one cannot respond to this kind of desert experience with morality or with the demand that a person should persevere. He argues that pious discourses merely indicate mechanisms of flight that are intended to help us avoid a confrontation with emptiness.

The human being is fragile and imperfect, even when he lives together with another human being. It is inevitable, in this life together, that the partners begin to come unstuck because of their unrealistic ideas and ideals. Many couples react to this with disappointment, and abandon their relationship. Bellet, however, pleads for a greater realism here, which he calls "sobriety." This sobriety can lead the married partners to bid farewell to all their ideas and formulations about the ideal marriage and to say "yes" to a life together that is (more than) good enough, to say "yes" to a man or a woman who is (more than) good enough. We see already a success when the partners accept one another as "sufficient," love one another "sufficiently," and do no harm to the other. Mutual respect

thus becomes a primordial possibility that allows the partners also to survive periods of emptiness.

Love of Enemies and Humility

In the Gospel, we are promised that love is stronger than death. Love wants to check death and to give life in abundance: "I came that they may have life, and have it abundantly" (Jn 10:10). For Christians, there is a close link between living and loving. The Father of Jesus is love, the Father of Jesus is the creator and the liberator of all life. Everything that gives life comes from love. Love protects life. Love wants the other to live genuinely. Love challenges the other to live. Love says "yes" to the unique, imperfect life of the other. Love gives acceptance and blessing.

It is not easy here to accept the other with his or her otherness, although it is often affirmed that this is essential to a relationship of love. This is because the other not only appears as fascinatingly other (*fascinosum*) and thereby as one who challenges me to pursue my own growth. Rather, the other is also experienced as hostile (*tremendum*). The desire of the other, which is an obstacle and even a threat to my own desire, terrifies me. But if I attempt to neutralize the desire of the other, I fail to do justice to him. Instead, I do violence to him. Another possibility is to give unchecked admittance to the hostile desire. I then allow myself then to be colonized by that which is foreign to me. But this fails to do justice to me, and I thereby allow someone to do violence to me.

The Golden Rule affirms: "Do to others as you would have them do to you" (Lk 6:31; see also Mt 7:12). When Jesus invites us to love our enemies, all that he is doing is to apply this Golden Rule consistently. Ultimately, we expect of our enemies that they will lay down their weapons and respect us and love us. This is

why Jesus invites us to do exactly the same: namely, to respect and to love our enemies. This does not entail integrating the hostile desire of the other uncritically, but acknowledging with respect and love the desire of the other as something that is justified. We are invited to acknowledge the desire for life both in the hostile desire of the other and in our own selves, and to find out what will be life-giving for both partners in the relationship.

If this is to succeed, however, more is required than scholarship alone. Rather, we must part company with our theories and ideologies about life and love. The decisive point here is that true love affects the entire person. True love is the gift of life to the full – and this gift, like the birth of a child, is bestowed only after intense birth pangs. A perverted and superficial notion of love generates both the idea of a painless self-sacrifice and the attempt to force another person to love one. These two strategies disregard the imperfection of the human being and undermine a relationship that is based on equality. The outcome is a caricature of that which gives life. It is love that creates life, and love is itself complete and utter gift. No matter how intense one's desire may be, it cannot compel the other to love. Love can only be a gift from the one who loves. This is why Maurice Bellet pleads not only for a great realism, but also for great humility in love. He believes that we touch the transforming power of love inwardly only when we have had the courage to work existentially, and on the level of the relationship, through the hard work of the love of enemies, and when (both in regard to the other and in regard to our own self) we respond to the threat of inhumanity with humaneness, to the threat of hatred with respect, and to the threat posed by violence with the decision we take in favor of that which gives life.

Struggle and Divine Meekness

How are those who love to hold out against these threats, and where are they to find the strength for a confrontation of this kind? Some manage to do so through their own efforts, but most people need reliable persons who stay the course with them and give support, consolation, and hope. They need people who do not break the bruised reed or quench the glimmering wick (see Is 42:3). These friends bear witness to that which is wholly other, namely, to the love that is stronger than death and that encompasses more than the love of the marriage partners.

The divine meekness can become visible through the important decision in favor of more humaneness and more life. This divine meekness is the love that lays down no conditions. In the presence of this love, I am permitted to be as I am. In this divine meekness there lies the experience that one has already been accepted in one's deepest inner dimension. In the light of this transcending presence, it is possible for a room to come into existence in which those who love can come together in an unexpected openness. With their vulnerability, they stand both alongside one another (*fascinosum*), even if in a tentative and hesitant manner, and over against one another (*tremendum*). The words that are spoken in this room of divine meekness are freed from illusions, and unveil the imperfect human being. This unveiling constitutes an initiation into the mystery of the divine love.

The divine love is linked all too frequently, even today, with perfection, with a continuously intensive experiencing and a transcending of all that is earthly. But Christians are familiar with other sides of God too. They believe that God became a human being in Jesus, who shared with us his own path of love and suffering, and was therefore raised up by God to new life. It is our imperfect being that became the place of our redemption (as Ter-

tullian says, *caro salutis cardo,* "The flesh is the hinge on which salvation hangs"), since, in Jesus, God has loved our imperfection and elevated it to divinity.

In their attempt to transcend limitations, those who love sooner or later come up against their boundaries. Living together is often laborious, and the otherness of one's partner is experienced acutely. We are conscious that love is fragile; but in this case, those who are sacramentally married are summoned to hold fast to the "yes" they have said. They are to say "yes" to the imperfection of the other, because otherwise, life is not possible. Being human means allowing each other to live, instead of attacking each other's life. Being human in the image of God means, in fact, allowing each other to live the life that is imperfect and limited. Against the background of the inextinguishable "yes" of the divine meekness, Christians believe that through their own "yes," even vulnerability and imperfection can become the origin of life and of grace.

Gift and Gratitude

Through the experience of the divine meekness, the partners can set in a new context the path that they have taken together. When they look back on the past, they see the mustard seeds that were sown along the curving path through life. Mustard seeds are very small, but they have the potential for a great harvest. The smallest word and the slightest gesture of humaneness are now filled (so to speak) with divine meekness. In these sacred moments in the history of the married couple, they are summoned to new life by means of visible and effective signs. What they bestow on each other in these moments is not something they themselves can produce. Rather, it comes to them as a gift, and they receive it as a grace. "Grace" means here that they are permitted to experience

that they can be a source of joy and protection not only for God, but also for each other.

Gratitude for this grace can come into being only when it is not seen as something to be taken for granted. It requires the insight that a gift is involved here, and that the origin of all that is good lies outside one's own person. In that case, I experience that the other not only can challenge (*fascinosum*) or frustrate (*tremendum*) my desire, but that he can also encounter my desire in a friendly manner (*benevolens* – with benevolence) and can accommodate it in all its imperfection. Through gratitude, I learn that, despite everything, I receive much that is good, and that the wish of the other is that I should truly live. At the same time, I can recognize, in the gratitude of the other, that I can see his or her vulnerability. Despite all our imperfection, therefore, we can hand on life as partners, and be a sign of the divine meekness.

Desire and Ecstasy

Since gratitude demands both contemplation and insight, it is an experience that can lead to transformation. Those who love possess an insight that can make them become new human beings: namely, that the divine meekness is present in them too, and surrounds them everywhere. They can discover that despite their imperfections, they are lovable and capable of love. It is possible to give a new form and shape to the whole of their history and to the path they have taken together, with all the negative and positive experiences.

Through the experience of being loved by Love itself, one's own desire grows to help the other person's desire for life to unfold further. This desire for the other person's desire for life is ecstasy – literally, a "stepping out of oneself." This is a passionate and also painful desire to bestow life, and this desire is itself al-

ready life-giving. This strong desire never exists automatically or definitively. It remains imperfect; but at the same time, it is more than "good enough."

Married persons are called to deal with each other in a divinely meek and a grateful manner in the good times and in the bad times of their life together. By seeking ways to accept the other in his or her otherness, one succeeds in accepting oneself and becoming "imperfectly happy." It may at first sight appear paradoxical, but one's commitment to the life of the other nourishes one's own life as well.

This lasting commitment to the other person's desire for life is not the same thing as the wish to protect the other person in his or her vulnerability. The partners feel attracted by the strength and the greatness of the other, and want to support and stimulate these qualities. They challenge one another to become a "sufficiently good" human being.

The partners remain a mystery to each other, since they are continually revealing themselves and withdrawing from each other. The various phases in a relationship ensure that the divine meekness takes on ever new expressions. The period of intense infatuation passes into the daily dealings with the partner with whom one is familiar. The education of children poses the next challenge to the relationship. The middle-aged phase is characterized by the partners' search for more authenticity in their life together. In old age, the partners have a greater need of care. Married people are challenged again and again to deal with their own imperfection, and that of their partner, in a way that is life-giving. In order that this path of especial intimacy can succeed, courage, imagination, patience, gentleness, power, and trust are required.

Conclusion

Robert Walser writes: "One who does not love, has no existence. He does not exist, he is dead. One who desires to love arises from the dead. Only the one who loves is alive." Gabriel Marcel puts this as follows: "To love someone means saying: ‚You will not die'." Love wants to break the threat and the curse of death, since love is full of passion for the life of the other. In marriage, Christians daily share with body and soul the life, the death, and the resurrection of Jesus Christ. Their commitment and their suffering can bring forth new life. All we can do is to react with astonishment and quiet thankfulness.

Notes

[1] M. BELLET: *Le paradoxe infini,* Paris: Desclée de Brouwer, 2004.

Marriage: Mystery within the Mundane

Annette Barker

Marriage is a human institution. It is a natural state, entered into within every form of human tribe, group or religion. "Between husband and wife friendship seems to exist by nature for man is naturally disposed to pairing."[1] The question rises, then, how can it be known that the mystery of God's love is operating in marriage? For the authentic interpretation of the mystery of God in the mundane is itself a challenge. Yet from a faith perspective it can be acknowledged that the action of God is revealed in the mundane activities of everyday life, from the smallest daily event to the most significant situation. It is a matter of faith that God is with us as we attempt to stay with God. St. Paul proclaims this mystery of Christ (Col. 1:24-27 and 4:3)[2] and this proclamation continues today as ordinary married Christians quietly and often privately acknowledge the presence of God in their married lives.

The process of interpreting the presence of God is not presumption – but hope that God is in the mundane, for where else can God be? The mundane, therefore, becomes sacred, a sacredness which is continually creative. In some mysterious way the married couple share in the Trinity. As a child I was taught about the mystery of the Trinity. The nuns told us that God the Father loved Jesus Christ so much that the love itself between Father and

Son became the Holy Spirit. In my childish way I pondered this statement. I found it quite easy to accept this explanation for the love in my home between my parents was a reality. When I visited other homes and families, in comparison to my home, the atmosphere was cold and unloving. It seemed to me that the space between husband and wife is a sacred holy space, regardless of the absence or presence of a child. The space between the couple is not made holy because children are created. It is holy because it is the interaction of the two people who themselves are trying to become more God like. Creativity is operating continuously, in an environment where the individuals develop towards God, becoming the person God designed them to be. This is happening to both husband and wife and it is in this context that as both individuals interact, the interaction itself becomes sacred and the home becomes a sacred space – holy ground. The home is the sacred space for fulfilling destinies and potential. God is present in the "in-between-ness" of the husband and wife. The couple integrate the authentic message of Christ within their heart and mind to allow the graced aspects of their behaviour to reflect their inner Christ like disposition. If both are attempting to live in a personally Christ centred way then there will be an energy between them which might be considered to be akin to the power of the Holy Spirit which proceeds from the Father and Son. This action is revealed in the mundane activities of everyday life.

Within this holy ground husband and wife learn to trust each other, from the fledgling beginnings of the early courtship, to the end days. They learn to trust the other with their lives and their very souls, helping each other along the path that leads to eternity. As God trusted humanity with creation (Gn 1:22-28) so husband and wife trust each other with their future. (Gn 2:18-25.) God and the couple enter into a partnership. Now, the mystery of God's

trust in humanity is being revealed in the ordinariness of every day life. God trusts us with the creation.

Every Day Life

God continuously reveals the creative nature of love in the microscopic movements of daily life. This love from God enfolds all the comings and goings in the home. Through this movement a wonderful discovery of the other person takes place. And in the context of trust it is then possible for both husband and wife to risk self disclosure of the deepest part of their being. The friendship and confidence in each other reflect the confidence that God had when creation was first entrusted into the hands of humanity.

There are wonderful opportunities to practice virtue – hidden virtues known only to God, allowing God's grace to act like the refiners fire, shaping, pruning, challenging and encouraging virtuous growth in both partners. There are situations when in losing emphasis on self-interest and focusing on the other's interest the matrimonial bond is maintained.

The friendship grows and a community of love develops over the years, so that because of the community element, no marriage is isolated from the broader Christian community. Jesus Christ stated "For where two or three meet in my name I am there among them." (Mt 18:20) This promise applies to all those marriages where God is invited in.

This promise may be in times of joy. It can equally be in times of great distress, sadness, neglect and divorce. God's commitment to stay in relationship with us is reinforced when Christ says, "I am with you always, yes, to the end of time" (Mt 28:20). This includes to all those who in some way or other have entered into a partnership with God, including those who make solemn promises at the altar regardless of the success or not of the subsequent

marriage. Many married couples attempt to fulfil their original promises, but for a multitude of reasons, which are not the subject of this essay, this is not possible. For others there is a continuous striving to love the other unconditionally and to imitate God's love within marital love.

The careful balance between utter self giving and self realisation is a challenge which is met when both husband and wife, are sensitive to the needs of the other. Jesus Christ's exemplary example of how to live a fully human life, infused with the divine is held out to Christians as the way to live. Christ was able to do this: to give himself completely for others and in so doing to fulfil himself. The challenge for the married couple is follow Christ's example and to do it in tandem with another: to be self giving and self fulfilled. It seems to me that it is precisely where the paradox of modern marriage lies.

Mansfield and Collard in their study examine the process of becoming a couple yet together remaining separate. The experience of sixty five couples is analysed. Mansfield and Collard state that:

> Despite the promise of emotional fulfilment offered by modern marriage, the gender gap of expectation in many of these newly-wed marriages was wide and men seem either to be unaware of this or unable to accept it. Wives, in contrast acknowledged the existence of the gap and hoped to bridge it. There is it seems "his" marriage and "her" marriage existing apart from their marriage.

Later they conclude that:

> To allow oneself to be seduced by the notion of the couple as a symbiotic union, and regard then as an undifferentiated pair, is to miss the essential difference in marriage – the heterogeneity of the spouses: men and women are different. Modern marriage is a para-

> dox. The language of marital relationships denies difference; the reality of married life defies sameness.[3]

Thatcher draws attention to the different roles within marriage and states that:

> A husband and a wife are simultaneously a person, a partner and (probably at some time) a parent. Attending to one another's needs in all three roles might constitute the first basic task of marital spirituality.[4]

Juggling the roles that Thatcher cites demands a marital spirituality which applies the Gospel message, imitates Christ and articulates Kingdom values. St. Paul's letter to the Galatians, particularly 5:13-26 and 6:1-10 can provide tools for living within a Christian marriage, particularly where only the impossible seems possible. For love and the will to love are closely linked. By bringing the intellect and the will to bear on marital situations, God's grace is given another avenue through which to act.

Daily in marriage there are hundreds of opportunity to let Christ increase and ourselves decrease. The opportunities to practice love come in small moments. There may be nothing whatsoever grand about the smallest act of kindness yet it is in this minute moment that God reveals himself by sustaining that moment with his support graciously given. Each person has the chance to cheerfully subjugate their own needs and demands, to go the extra mile (Mt 5:41) to suppress the irritable retort, to see a comment from the other view point, to put up with a persistent habit, and at the same time to know ones own strength, value and significance so that balance and equality exist and no one is either a door mat or dominated or domineering. Thinking of the others' needs without losing one's own identity is demonstrated by Jesus Christ when he cooked the apostles' breakfast after his resurrec-

tion, anticipating the fishermen's needs .What an example! A God who cooks breakfast! (Jn 21:9-14). With an example from Christ like this, in marriage we can also be alert to the unspoken needs of the other.

Challenges: Pain and Suffering

In life there are many times when the mundane is saturated with pain and suffering. There is disharmony caused by personality clashes, differing needs, or challenging circumstances. Loneliness caused from different demands. The man or women may need to work to maintain the home, the children may need attention simply because they need nurturing or because they are sick. The couple may be so busy doing their duty that they have little time for each other. There can be sense of abandonment and isolation within marriage. All one partner may desire for support and comfort is the physical presence of the other to share an interest, a conversation or just pick up a tea towel to do the drying up together. The other partner is always pre-occupied with other matters declaring at the same time "Well, I'm working for the family," "I'm caring for our children". There seems no room whatever for precious moments to stop and just be together as a couple. Perhaps that is why Jesus enjoyed Mary's company when he declared she had chosen the better part – she simply stopped and was present to Jesus and he to her (Lk 10:38-42). There is a place for this companionship within the normal married life and Jesus appreciated that point. Many people are like Martha living busy lives: there is necessity for both but to maintain relationships time needs to be given to being present as completely as possible to the other. Both may long for companionship and comfort, but the other is too weary and preoccupied to enter into the other's loneliness. Jesus longed for the supportive companionship of Peter, James and

John. (Mt 26:38-43). He was suffering such an agony, an agony he needed support for. No such support was forthcoming. Three times he asked, three times he continued to hope that his needs would be acknowledged, yet, each time he was disappointed. This scenario repeats itself in marriage many times. Jesus also has been left isolated, alone suffering and distressed. The pain he felt is felt by married people as they grapple with pain and isolation within marriage. Both may say: "Could you not stay one hour with me." (Mt 26:38-43).

An angel of the Lord we are told finally assisted Jesus. (Lk 22:43). Only God could sustain Jesus' intolerable burden. In this there is another aspect that is crucial to appreciate in Christian marriage and that is that, in the depth of the individual, despite the shared companionship of marriage, there are times when God alone can support the individual. We cannot be God for each other. In marriage it is necessary to allow the mystery of God's love to operate uniquely in the heart and mind of the individual as well as between the couple.

Husbands and wives may be pulled in all directions at once: towards each other, towards their children and increasingly pulled to care for two sets of elderly ailing parents. During these times it is hard to hold on to the idea that God is in this demanding muddle. One man with a precociously demanding ninety six year old mother living with him and his wife, a grandson with cystic fibrosis and stressed daughter, said when he himself was diagnosed with Leukaemia: "God has forgotten us." Christ's words echo through the ages into the heart of the domestic situation. "My God, My God, why have you forsaken me?"(Mt 27:46).

Intimate Space

Paradoxically, the disastrous situation is also the place of healing and resurrection. "Marriage", St. Augustine of Hippo states, "is not when limbs are locked but when hands are held."[5] One crucial dimension of marriage is that of ongoing healing. In the Gospel there are many examples of Jesus' healing touch. He had bodily contact with those in distress. Jesus healed then, and now, he continues to enter into healing relationships, through the mystery of his love. Inner healing is available to both husband and wife, to heal the hurts from the past and from the ongoing hurts that occur in normal living .The intimate relationship encompasses the capacity to offer consolation, tenderness, and understanding in times of desolation and misery as well as in times of happiness and joy. This healing can be expressed physically. The human act of intercourse becomes the place of divine action – an action which includes more than procreation. St. Augustine states, "Just don't undervalue the intercourse of two hearts entwined."[6] The mystery of God enters through our entwined hearts and bodies. God is in the ordinary acts of caring living, and in the sexual act itself.

God is present in the pleasure of sexual expression, delighting in the fulfilment of each person who can feel very near to God when involved in sexual intercourse. Intimacy with each other allows God to be intimate with the individual and is present within the intimacy between the couple. God is mysteriously present in the "inbetweeness" of the couple. The mundaneness of marriage is infused with the mystery of God.

Notes

[1] ARISTOTLE: Nicomachean Ethics 8.12, as quoted in J.F. CHILDRESS J./J. MACQUARRIE (eds.): *A New Dictionary of Christian Ethics*, London: SCM Press, 1986, 366.

[2] Quotations of the Bible from: *The New Jerusalem Bible*, London: Darton Longman & Todd, 1994.

[3] P. MANSFIELD/J. COLLARD: *The Beginning of the Rest of Your Life? A Portrait of Newly-wed Marriage*, Basingstoke: Macmillan, 1988, 179.

[4] A. THATCHER: *Marriage after Modernity: Christian Marriage in Postmodern Times*, Sheffield: Sheffield Academic Press, 1999, 214.

[5] AUGUSTINE OF HIPPO: *Sermons to the People*, ed. and transl. W. Griffin, New York: Doubleday, 2002, 32 (Sermo LI).

[6] Ibid.

Time and Marriage

Alfons Vansteenwegen

This article is about time in a marriage relationship. Partners differ in their perception of time. How can they create time for really being together? We will talk about the past and the future of the relationship. And about time as a requisite for good sex! We conclude with a number of tips for a good use of time in the marriage relationship.

In speaking here of time, we are not referring to time measured by the clock. Clock time is nicely clear-cut and nicely divided into equal segments: hours, minutes, and seconds. We want here to speak of time as we perceive it. In our perception, time sometimes passes quickly, at other times more slowly. When visiting the dentist, a quarter of an hour can seem like hours. When we are lost in a good book, fifteen minutes have gone before we know it! Nor do we always perceive time as being linear. Some people still have bits of their past that get in their way. When someone experiences a trauma, they may be burdened with it for a long time. In this discussion we will consider time as we perceive it, not the time of the clock.

Partners Differ in their Perception of Time

Partners living together differ in their perception of time. Let us identify a number of these differences.

Difference in tempo. One of the partners may be able to carry out tasks much more quickly than the other. If he vacuums, then it does not take as much time as when she does it.

Difference in punctuality. For a couple, eight o'clock is never eight o'clock. He wants to be there at ten minutes to eight, she is happy to get there at half past.

A difference in time orientation. He is still full of the last vacation; she is already planning the next one.

Difference in reaction time. She immediately becomes furiously angry, but ten minutes later has forgotten all about it. He does not get very angry, but broods for months on an incident and brings it up time and time again.

Research has demonstrated that men respond much more heatedly and much longer physically. Their heartbeat, for example, needs much more time to return to normal. This may be the reason why men put up a wall, withdraw, and stop responding during arguments.

Difference in the time required to process issues. He can put a mishap with the children behind him immediately. She continues to suffer from it for years. She cannot keep quiet about it.

A difference in how one plans time. She plans time together in advance. He lives with the attitude "we will see what turns up." After all, she takes care of everything!

Difference in the desired frequency. As a couple, we differ time and time again in how often we want to do something. This is true especially in the area of sex. But in actual fact, we differ in the desired frequency of so many things: going for a walk, watching television, etcetera.

Difference in intensity. One of the most important differences in dealing with time is the way in which we experience the day's rhythm. There are morning people and evening people. John is an early bird; he is remarkably boisterous and noisy while Mary eats her breakfast half asleep. But, when Mary is all ready to go in the evening, John is stretched out on the sofa asleep.

Couples also differ in the amount of sleep they require. Seldom do two partners require the same number of hours sleep.

To put it briefly, partners perceive time differently. This has significant consequences for their relationship.

Genuine Time Together cannot be found, it has to be created.

In light of the above, it becomes apparent that two partners each live in a different time zone. How can they then make sure that they have time together? Time together is not to be found. Time together has to be created. It is an achievement. To truly have time together, it has to be reserved in advance.

With "genuine time together" we here mean the time during which both partners are genuinely taken up with each other. Both are then 100 percent aware that they are with the other. Each is focused on the other.

These moments of time together may also become a ritual: every Saturday, John and Mary take time after lunch to sit and talk through the week that has just passed and to discuss the week to come. They do more than just compare their schedules. They share with each other what is on their heart. They listen intensely to each other. They feel with each other. These are the moments in which they realize that they are a couple. These are moments of intense relationship.

When couples want intimacy, they have to slow down. Intimacy requires the exchange of feelings and this always requires a slackening of pace. One has to identify one's feelings, articulate them and express them to one's partner. The partner seeks to identify with the other. This is however not the same as "feeling the same way." Genuine affinity is putting oneself into the other's shoes and giving weight to their partner's feelings. This cannot take place rapidly! It requires time. Every deep, shared experience in the relationship demands that one slows down. Deceleration is what is needed here.

The Past in One's Marriage

It is not because partners experience life together that they also have a shared past. All true sense of togetherness experienced by a couple only develops through communication. The past can only become a shared past if the couple talks about it every so often. An important point here is bringing closure to any painful experience that has taken place between the partners. One partner has hurt the other. How can they both get over it? Not by acting as though nothing has happened, for people do not forget. It could be dealt with in this way: Mary explains to John how much she has been hurt by his behaviour. John shows and communicates that he understands how difficult it must have been for her. Then John explains to Mary how the mishap came about and what his intention had been. In her turn, Mary tries to understand this. John subsequently says he is sorry for what he has put her through. Together they decide to bury the wound. Then they do something enjoyable together as an initiative toward a new future together.

The Future in a Marriage

Partners always begin their marriage with the idea that it will be forever. A lasting relationship is something precious in life. But this demands that partners make plans for the future in light of one other. They need to reach agreement about the goals of their life together. A relationship lived together is not just a question of feelings. Feelings pass. The feeling of being in love is temporary, everybody knows that. Every relationship has periods during which the feelings for each other diminish or die out. One finds oneself temporarily in a neutral state toward the other. This is why commitment is necessary. Commitment means: being prepared to make sacrifices for the other. Commitment has to do especially with behaviour, not so much with words. Commitment exists in the relationship itself, in the attention one has for the other, in the time one is prepared to make for the other, in everything that one does for the other, without further thought. In order to evaluate a relationship, one should not go on the feelings of the moment. Evaluating a relationship demands that one considers one's feelings about the relationship and how much effort one has put into the relationship over a longer period of time.

Sex Requires Time

In marriage relationships, sexuality plays an important role. During the period of being in love, sex is spontaneous. But later on in the relationship, good sex is something that both parties need to work at. Furthermore, for good sex, time is necessary. Good sex demands that one knows a little in advance that there is a possibility that sex might be on the agenda and have sufficient time to invest in it. A quickie is of course always an option once in a while, but this should be the exception. Moreover, the woman

often needs more time to feel in the mood for sex than the man. People do not like to make concrete plans ahead of time for when they are going to have sex, that somewhat robs sex of its spontaneity. However, on the other hand, it becomes apparent time and again that if no mention has been made beforehand, it "very often does not happen." So, to truly make love together, it is necessary to take each other into account. For it is usually one partner who is the first to want to have sex. The other is not yet in the mood. Having sex together then always involves the overcoming of a difference.

Tips for Managing Time in a Relationship Lived out Together

Are there any other tips for a good use of time in a love relationship? Certainly!

Whenever partners differ in what they want, and when a compromise or an acceptable alternative is not possible, then one can choose to take turns. This time we will do what I want to do, and next time we can do what you want to do. Then, in turn, we will both have what we really want.

In a relationship it is important that each partner has some time in which he or she can be left alone in peace. We call this an "island." The more time one has together, the more often one needs time on an island, however paradoxical that sounds.

A commitment is only a commitment if it is bound to a particular time. If no time has been fixed, then a commitment is incomplete. Many partners make a declaration of intent, but this is not a commitment. "We should take more exercise" is not a commitment. A commitment is: "Every Sunday, between two and four o'clock, we are going to take a walk, whatever the weather!"

Whoever lives alone can afford not to make plans. But with two people, one *must* plan, since otherwise it will be impossible to do things together. Everything that one wishes to do together needs to be determined together beforehand. In a relationship, it is better to arrange things in advance than to have to make adjustments in retrospect.

When both partners return home from work, then a so-called "decompression chamber" is very useful. We mean by this that on coming home, each person can do a few things for themselves and in this way prepare him/herself again for interaction. He takes time to go through the post and to flick through the newspaper, and she goes and gets changed in the bathroom or takes a shower.

Every couple has to invest a minimum of time in their relationship. Apart from "me time," there also has to be a "we time." Whoever does not make time for the other, will come to lose the other. Three quarters of an hour a week to catch up with each other is no luxury, but a necessity!

In Conclusion:

Marriage partners differ in their perception of time. Genuine time together demands an effort. This time is necessary in order to bridge the many differences encountered in living together. Attention has also been given to the way in which partners establish a shared past and a joint future. In closing, a number of practical tips were summarized. Both time on one's own and time with each other is important. Intimacy always requires that one slows down and takes the time to be with and give one's full attention to the other. Time is then an exceptional dimension of living together and of loving each other.

The Art of Growing Old: Paths to the Inner Acceptance of the Inexorable Process of Aging

Aldegonde Brenninkmeijer-Werhahn

It is not easy to write credibly about old age; this can be done only by one who has acquired a certain experience of old age. In this essay, I should like to hand on to the next generation, "from heart to heart," something that has been acquired and tried out in twenty-three years of experience with INTAMS (International Academy for Marital Spirituality) and in the 45th autumn of our married life.

Reflection on aging shows us that there are various attitudes and inclinations in each age group. For example, there are the *hope* and the *confidence* that we will be able to get old together; the *serenity* that comes of no longer having to stand under the usual pressure and to keep pace with others, as one gets older; the *endeavor* to face up to the contemporary situation appropriately and continually, even when this is not always easy; the *readiness* to exchange experiences with other age groups; and the *inner wish* to be questioned about the treasure of one's own experience and to be understood by the younger generation.

These hopeful expectations are only one side of the coin. We also find disappointment and bitterness. For example, there is the unacknowledged *refusal* to accept one's own age and the compulsive need to be always young; this can go as far as feelings of jealousy towards those who are in fact young. There are *resentments* against all that is new and strange; or there is a *claim to absolute authority* in relation to those who are younger. As a reaction to this, it is the younger ones who want to remain among themselves and who exclude the older person, or even meet him with disdain. Behind this lies the fear of not being accepted – and this fear exists on both sides, among both young and old.

Among the active generation, who do not yet have any practice in getting old, there is also a mental attitude that sees the process of aging as not in any way "venerable." Aging does not look like something one would want to imitate; nor is it a warning sign. But the older person has an important task in relation to those whose life is waxing: he should present himself with grace, charm, and humor, in a dignified, honorable, and respectable manner, in order to counteract the subtle hostility to those whose life is waning.

Critical Questions about an Aging Society

Sacred scripture relates that Methuselah reached the fabulous age of nine hundred and sixty-nine years. No matter how we may evaluate this computation of time, the trend in the modern industrial nations is unambiguous. Every ninth person in the world today is aged sixty or more. The Population Division of the United Nations predicts that in 2050, every fifth person will be over sixty. At the present day, the number of older persons is higher in the developed countries. In Europe, every fifth person is already over sixty; in Asia, Latin America, and the Caribbean, every tenth person is over sixty; and in Africa, every nineteenth person. Nevertheless,

the population in the developing countries is aging more quickly than in the industrial countries, in which the age of the population is already higher.

From today's perspective, it is disturbing to note that this is accompanied by a steep decline in births in the western hemisphere. This draws attention more and more to the old person. Medical science is acquiring a more exact knowledge of how to care for the old person, and it develops gerontological therapies. We also know more and more about the various causes of death, so that it is easier to combat these. Social care is also creating ever better conditions that make it possible to live longer. But how do we deal with the elderly, when they become a financial problem? What about the pensions that must be paid, the health care, and the need for places in nursing homes and for care attendants? More and more voices are being raised to question how human and humane our society is, and how legislation can protect the weakest members in our society. What answer and help can the Christian faith give us? The health spokesmen of the political parties praise all the progress in medicine, therapy, and care, but this is still far from answering the question of how I can inwardly accept my old age. Behind the growing need for help, dependence on others, and being overlooked because of one's weak position, there lie hidden bitter experiences and great challenges to the elderly person, to families, to doctors and caring personnel, and to the state and the Churches. What answers do we have for the person who is growing old, if he "merely suffers" his aging? How can one prepare for a meaningful aging process?

The Marriage Covenant and its Meaning for Growing old Together

The beginning and the end of life are mysterious things. The beginning of a life, with birth and childhood, leads via becoming adult to the point when the arc of life declines, and one day comes to a stop. Between these poles lie moving segments of life that one does not simply leave behind one. Rather, they accompany one through life like a *cantus firmus*. The spaces in each segment of life that are filled up become in turn a composition that spreads out over the course of life and becomes a unique composition of "oneself." Life is not composed of independent, juxtaposed parts. Life forms a whole, the parts of which always remain present in the overall course of life. This becomes particularly clear in the case of marriage. Here, we have two original melodies with two different sequences of notes, which belong to two life stories that want to come together, in order to follow a plan for life together and to write the *common* history of a marriage.

The marriage covenant presupposes that the married partners remain together and that their perspective of a lengthy life (sometimes for sixty years and more) holds fast. What attitude do married partners, who want to accompany each other through life as faithful companions, take to this – in a world that, like a supermarket of the modern age, promises that dreams of perfection, beauty, and success will be fulfilled, and all desires will be satisfied? What is then the power of the married promise that husband and wife make to each other: "Do you wish to go with me through life in good times and in bad, until death do us part?" More and more married partners today are asking: "How do I keep our marriage fresh, even if we are to reach the age of a Methuselah?"

The course of married life is exposed to trials of every kind: the first independent steps taken by the children, until they leave

their parents' home; professional changes, or even dismissal and the loss of employment; the double professional career of husband and wife; retiring from the world of work; childlessness; biological and physical changes, especially in the wife; the differing irritability of the partners; sickness; a handicapped child, or even the death of a child; religious differences. The sexologist Alfons Vansteenwegen puts it in a nutshell in the title of his book: *Love is a verb*.

Many a marriage is put to the test early on. The development as a couple can face great tests and challenges, and the marriage partners must reflect seriously on how they can work on their life together, in order to fill it with content in the long term. Equality can be an important factor that helps to guard against a subtle corrosion of the female and male character. The marital orientation to one another in differing gender roles is important, in order to keep open possibilities of development. An open and honest communication between the partners is an essential factor in marriage, and requires special training even into one's old age. This helps us to build up a basis of reciprocal trust and reliability. That is also the context in which one can put into words what troubles one, and to practice the virtue of accepting one another and of long-lasting renunciation. But what binds all this together in marriage is faith in God and trust in God. It is here that the church in the fellowship of the home begins. The Second Vatican Council called this the "domestic church."

Handing on to the Coming Generation what has been acquired and tested

Everyone longs deeply to hand on personally important insights in the family, in school, in youth groups, in the churches, and in society, since a conversation is an encounter in which the *word* and

hearing come together in the same way. No communication via Twitter, Facebook, or SMS attains the significance of a personal, oral conversation in which insightful experiences can be handed on. When one is alone, one experiences chiefly a dissatisfaction, when something important remains shut up inside oneself. What a joy it is, then, when this inner sphere is allowed to open up in order to share with one or several other persons the wealth of questions, problems, and hopes that one has experienced! In a self-centered society, this applies especially to the married state. In the course of time there may develop a stronger wish to remain on one's own, not to have to give an account of oneself, not to be pestered with questions. This is the moment when a dilemma opens up between liberation and breathing freely, on the one hand, and the wish to communicate oneself to one's partner, on the other. We encounter here a central dilemma, which consists in finding over the course of the years of married life a synthesis that does justice both to the desire to communicate and to respect for the intimate, inner sphere.

A story in Michel Tournier's book *The Midnight Love Feast (Le médianoche amoureux: Contes et nouvelles)* is apposite here. In this book, we meet a married couple who are drawn from life. After some years of marriage, they have nothing more to say to each other. They believe that they know each other well enough; the partner no longer offers anything new. Life together is boring, and it is high time to change one's partner. They now experience a great deal of friction every day, and they have lost the ability to understand the partner. But before they part company, they decide to invite their friends one last time, in order to communicate their decision to them towards the end of the evening. In order to give this evening a structure, they ask each guest to tell a moving story from his or her own life after supper. When the last story has been told, the hosts are so deeply impressed that they resolve

to continue the marriage they have begun. The evening meal thus turns into a love feast. The two experience how inexhaustible and unique is the reservoir of profound experiences in each human being, and how it is still possible to discover undiscovered paths in the other. They realize ever more clearly how painful the experience of a separation is, when this simply abrogates the covenant of the process of married life in their common growth. For it is only as one gets older, that one discovers the meaning of the years that one has lived in the past.

But the couple in the story also have the valuable and helpful experience of fellowship, and they learn the important significance that the marital fellowships of the others can have for their own marriage. This shows how helpful a fellowship with friends can be. Here, confidential memories are exchanged, and people learn to understand each other better. This too belongs to the treasure of experience that can be exchanged credibly and handed on only in the word and in hearing.

Some Foundations on which a Culture of Conversation can be built up in Marriage and the Family

First of all, there is the honest will to establish a basis for mutual *trust* and the inner wish to anchor more deeply in faith the promise that was made before God at the altar, even after 25 and more years of marriage.

There are some basic questions that can provide support for the culture of conversation in marriage. The progression of the various phases of marriage also includes the necessary provision for the retirement that will inevitably come one day. Every married couple must face this question, if they are to prepare in good

time a shared and happy autumn of their life. This is the life's work that belongs to every culture of marriage. What does one feel when one is dismissed from professional work? What new *tasks and goals* do we posit for ourselves, things that are personally fulfilling for me and for us and that can help us to cope together with retirement and to enrich it? The adage that a plough that no longer ploughs rusts quickly applies here too, and this is why it is an erroneous conclusion, when our western mentality simply "shelves" the experiences of many persons who have retired because of a law that stipulates this, instead of employing their skills and their knowledge for the common good, even if their work speed has become slower.

Another concern that ought to be discussed in the conversation between husband and wife is about the bodily constitution. The desire for everlasting youth can scarcely be underestimated; but our bodily organism is already in decline at the age of forty. This applies especially to a woman in her mature years. But the logo-psychologist Viktor Frankl asks in his book *Psychotherapie für den Laien* (*Psychotherapy for the Layperson*) whether we are not confusing *maturing* with *getting old.* Are not man and woman on the path to their spiritual peak, and to the high point in the biography of their personality, precisely when the slow biological "decline" begins? This time often comes when the children leave the house and dare to take their first independent steps. In this inevitable biological moment, the married partners are challenged anew to shoulder this task in different ways. In this moment, there is often an unsaid inner desire to be able to talk about the various feelings, in order to protect oneself against a separation that may be imminent; but they lack the ultimate willingness or the necessary help. This inner desire does not come automatically. The couple – both husband and wife – must work at it in good time. When one accompanies married couples, one frequently sees the

extra suffering they inflict on their married life as they part company, because they are no longer permitted to experience how what they have acquired together up to that point can come to maturity through another new beginning. And this means that they do not experience how the values that they have acquired blossom in fellowship.

Another useful practice is the recollection of the good years of the marriage in the past, the years that have helped again and again to cope with the present situation in life. The momentary situation is judged too easily and too quickly on the basis of the irrevocable *mistakes* that have been made. In order to get a new perspective on the present and the past, it is very important that the couple *make a shared investment in time.* This is not a waste of time; rather, it is precisely here that time is generated. The moments when the married partners regularly recall the good years of the past are irreplaceable and salutary. They find courage here to sketch out, step by step, the plan for their life in the shared years that lie ahead. In this situation, we are not acting like the prophet Jonah, who fled from God and from his task. The past is not something that no longer genuinely exists, and the future is not that which is not yet tangible. Rather, it is in the present that the past and the future are concentrated.

The Domestic Church: A Treasure of Experience in the Family

I should like to conclude by reflecting on the strength of the so-called "domestic church" and on the way in which this can take shape in marriage and family. In conversations with many couples who have been married for a long time, I experience again and again how they struggle with fidelity, with constancy in marriage, and with the gender-specific characteristics of the other partner.

One must seek again and again to come to a deeper reciprocal understanding, and see how this can be realized. Roger Schutz once said: "If a Christian credibly lives his profound conviction, even when this runs against the current of society, and keeps on searching for the inviolable fidelity of Christian married couples or for Christ's call to the purity of the unmarried state for the world, he can be certain that the seed that is thrown into the earth will germinate by day and by night." This seed is already enclosed in the sacrament of baptism, through which we enter into the covenant with God. The foundation stone is laid here, in order later to seal the friendship between a man and a woman before God at the altar as the covenant of marriage, so that they can become *one* community. In the First Letter of Peter (2:4-5), we read: "As living stones, let yourselves be built up to a spiritual house, to a holy priesthood." Karl Barth says that through baptism, we give glory to God and thus help to build up the Church of Jesus Christ. This is exactly what *ecclesia* means for every individual Christian: becoming a house of God. The Second Vatican Council took up this concept of the "spiritual house" as an important concept for the baptized layperson, in its document *Gaudium et spes,* 52. The concept of "domestic church" was taken up again in the Apostolic Exhortations *Familaris consortio* (1981), 21, and *Christifideles laici* (1988), 47. These church documents point out that the believing layperson, through his or her baptism, has a share in the threefold mission of Christ. We have received in baptism through Jesus Christ the *royal, priestly,* and *prophetic* mission. Every Christian is summoned thereby to become a holy and living temple of the Holy Spirit. The principle enunciated by Saint Paul, that "anyone who wishes to become one with Christ enters the sphere of the Spirit" (see 1 Cor 6:17), belongs absolutely to the spiritual self-consciousness of every believing layperson. In this sense, the domestic fellowship can become a fellowship of

prayer – and this requires training and practice over the years. This speaking with God can also bring a positive influence to bear on the culture of the marital conversation. It is here that the Church begins, when a domestic fellowship is lived spiritually in unity with God in the marital covenant and with the children and with the fellowship of humankind, in a royal, priestly, and prophetic manner. The family is summoned here to be a ray of hope for the others and to re-establish the order in the world again and again through trust, courage, fortitude, and reliability. This takes place in marriage and in family life, in daily work as well as in prayer and in study, in the task of education and in apostolic work, but also in leisure and in spare time, when these too are born of the Holy Spirit. It is here that marriage and the family fellowship become a shining sign that allows us to make our personal response to our vocation to be God's co-creators, through the fruits of the Holy Spirit, who has made us all witnesses of the risen Christ.

Biographical Perspectives and Experiences

Christian Marriage

Jack Dominian

The Roman Catholic tradition of marriage has one of the richest theologies of any Christian denomination and one of the poorest and least satisfactory pastorally experiences of all the sacraments of that Church. Nevertheless, in combination with the Eucharist, the People of God – overwhelmingly married – will live the bulk of their spiritual lives in this sacrament enjoying the fruits of its graces in this world and preparing themselves for their eternal destiny in the next. Thus, there is a sense of great urgency to really try to understand and appreciate the rich spontaneity present in it; and that is what I propose to do in this article.

The origin of this sacramental theology goes back to the 12th century. (In those days theological discussions took centuries; unlike the speed of modern communications.) Anyway, the great Reformer Luther did not believe that marriage was a sacrament and with a few words dismissed the notion saying that it was written nowhere in the Scriptures that it was so. As a result, the Council of Trent (1545 – 1563) defined it infallibly to be so, starting this sad difference between the Reformers and the Catholic Church which remains to this day.

Having defined marriage as a sacrament, the next question is "What brings it about?" Any church-going Catholic knows that

the majority of sacraments, especially the mass, are brought about by the presence and action of a priest.

Marriage is a singular exception and the first thing is to realise and appreciate, largely unknown by the vast majority of Catholics who get married, is the fact that it is "they" – the man and the woman – who confer this sacrament on each other. Because the confirming takes place in church with a priest and two witnesses in attendance, the couples naturally assume that the priest marries them. A natural mistake, but utterly wrong with immense spiritual implications as we shall see in a moment.

So the sacrament is conferred by the couple on each other, having assumed a lifelong, mutual commitment essentially of love. This commitment between each other is the heart of the sacrament but it is not the end of the story. The sacrament is "completed" with the first act of sexual intercourse. So then the sacrament is the combination of the mutual commitment coupled with sexual intercourse. And if coitus does not occur, then with the present laws of the Church, an unconsummated marriage can be annulled. (The Catholic Church does not recognise divorce but it does recognise annulment). Annulment is a big subject which is not of immediate concern to this article, so I will not deal with it any further.

I will now return to the theology of marriage. After several centuries with little change, the Second Vatican Council, some 50 years ago, made great and profound advances. It offered one of the shortest and important definitions of marriage which now has become a "community of life and love." For anyone really interested in the theology of marriage and the family, a full reading of the relevant text is certainly very rewarding.

Here I want to stress something very few married people realise which is that given its sacramental nature, spouses face and are in touch with Jesus Christ in each other throughout the whole

of their 24 hours of each day. This is an amazing and remarkable spiritual phenomenon.

The other common sacrament is the mass which after half to one hour is over. It is true that its graces extend beyond continuously in the life of those who attended it, but there is no such immediate encounter with Jesus Christ every second of their life.

When Catholics go to church, there is a feeling of wonder and awe as they become aware of the tabernacle where their living God is present. They genuflect and are aware of God in their midst.

The fact is that this is precisely what is happening all day long in each other's presence. Now the awe and wonder is part and parcel of their conversations, looking at each other's face, sitting together for a meal, hugging, stroking, and caressing each other. Every moment of their life is suffused with the presence of God. When we stop and think for a moment of this spiritual reality, it is amazing to realise that this is what Christian marriage is. Unfortunately no one, least of all the priest, makes couples aware of this fantastic spiritual fact.

But let us look at this a little bit more clearly. When spouses are chatting, we do not always understand and appreciate easily what we are saying to each other. There is need for patience to understand each other, tolerance at moments of being bored, or thinking of something else, or being distracted, even annoyed or angry. All this is an encounter of love as we struggle with the details of our human encounter. Invisibly but assuredly, God is present in the exchange and we experience the mystery of the Divine in each other with every word, look, or thought that takes place between us. We meet our God, in each other, every second.

We enter the church, dip our hand in holy water, and make the sign of the cross in preparation to meet God in the tabernacle. We come home, after a day's absence, and we greet each other and

equally we meet God. On entering the church, we genuflect in recognition of the God present in the tabernacle. At home, we sit down, start chatting, exchange news, become involved with each other, but in fact become engaged with God in each other.

The mystery of the Son of God who died on the Cross and resurrected three days later is present in the kitchen, in the sitting room, reading a letter or newspaper, attending to the children, preparing food, making the beds, exchanging the news of the day, through a kiss, a greeting, telling us if they have a headache, feel unwell, are on the phone, and so on. In all this, they are engaging with us. All normal, routine, ordinary, and yet all the time, utterly extraordinary because the unseen and invisible God is seen, heard, or touched through each other. In the sacrament of marriage the miracle of the ordinary is the transformation into something extraordinary.

One can understand why some people find all this description of the ordinary as being unworthy for the nature of a sacrament. We are accustomed to experiencing sacraments, the real presence of God in great cathedrals, and even the humblest church has a dignity of its own. But in marriage we are asked to experience the presence of almighty God in the midst of dirty floors, unclean dishes, dirty linen, the shouting and untidiness of young children, the chaos of the ordinary home. Not surprising that for some people, it is all too much of the mess of life.

And yet Mary, Joseph, and the baby Jesus did not turn their back on a stable; the presence of straw and a wide variety of animals with both shepherds and three kings paying homage to the Son of God.

The Church, even if it finds it difficult to write and describe what I am doing in this article, nevertheless has no hesitation in affirming that in the midst of this untold mess, the ordinariness of the home becomes the place of the encounter of the couple

with God in each other. If we stop to consider all this – the awe, the wonder, the magnitude of the extraordinary – becomes truly amazing.

For me, what is truly amazing is how little of all this is part and parcel of the understanding, appreciation, and realisation of the spirituality of the ordinary Catholic couple in their life. In our churches the light of the sanctuary lamp is the visible symbol of God's presence in the tabernacle. In the home, the couple are the light of God, present in each other in every corner of the house, in every niche of the home, a light that is never extinguished, burning bright with the grace (God's presence) with which illuminates the life of the couple.

The Second Vatican Council calls this "miracle" the domestic church – a word that needs much greater recognition and usage. Because in marriage it does not only make real the Divine presence in the domesticity of the couple but also adds an extra dimension for the words of Jesus who said "For where two or three meet in my name, I am there among them." (Mt 18:20)

The home – independently of its size, shape, contents, or quality – is where two or more of the baptised couple meet, with or without children, and that is precisely in this domestic church where Jesus is to be found. This reality is present every moment in the love of the family members.

So far, I have referred to the presence of love in the life of the couple and the family and yet anyone who has ever been such a member knows that family life is not all sweetness and light. There are tensions, arguments, and quarrels and a great heat can be generated in the midst of this sacrament. For anyone who is familiar with the life of Jesus and the scriptures, this should not be surprising. A picture of Jesus as sweet and mild does not correspond to the real Jesus.

He could be and was angry at times. He was angry in the tem-

ple when He went into it and drove all those who were sitting and buying there. He upset the money-changers and the seats of the dove setters. He said to them "According to scriptures my house will be called a house of prayer, but you are turning it into a bandits den." (Mt 21:12-14).

In the same way the ordinary home is usually a site and encounter of love but also tension, anger, and strife can be present. In these circumstances couples encountering God in each other have to act in the way He taught us how to cope with our anger. We have to forgive each other, not once, but repeatedly.

> Then Peter went up to him and said 'Lord, how often must I forgive my brother if he wrongs me? As often as seven times?' Jesus answered, "Not seven, I tell you, but seventy-seven times. (Mt 18:21)

The other side of the intimacy of the sacrament of marriage is conflict, and the other side of conflict is forgiveness. All this is taking place daily in the domestic church. The sacrament of marriage is not only a constant encounter of God with each other but there is the in-built structure of life, love, forgiveness, and reparation within the home. The confessional in the church can be used in exceptional circumstances but this unique sacrament of marriage has an in-built structure of much of the spiritual life of the couple.

At night, at the end of the day, the couple may or may not consummate further their love for each other through sexual intercourse. Sexuality has a long history of negativity in Christianity from the earliest centuries but it is worth reading what the Second Vatican Council has to say about it:

> The love of the (couple) expressed in their continuous encounter is uniquely expressed and perfected through the marital act. The actions within marriage by which the couple are united intimately and

> chastely are noble and worthy ones. Expressed in a manner which is truly human, these actions signify and promote the mutual self-giving by which spouses enrich each other with a joyful and a thankful will.

This is technical theological language describing what the overwhelming majority of married couples know as the pleasure of moving into their bedroom, taking pleasure in each other, undressing in each other's presence, and celebrating the mutuality of their bodies.

This bodily pleasure has a language of its own. On each occasion the couple are saying to each other, with or without words, at least five things:

– You are the most important person in my life, the person who I recognise, want, need, and appreciate. This now becomes, over a period of time, a most powerful affirmation of the identity (who we are) of the spouse.
– In intercourse the man confirms most powerfully the femininity of the woman and she does the same with the masculinity of her husband. It is a most powerful affirmation of their sexual identity (this is a point where homosexuality and heterosexuality diverge).
– I have already referred to the fact that couples quarrel. Usually they forget and forgive each other quickly, but sometimes the pain is deep and enduring. After an interval, sex often takes place. Here intercourse becomes a source of reconciliation and healing.
– Deep within us is the longing to feel wanted and of belonging which never goes away. After all, that is how we started life in the relationship with our mother. Sexual intercourse is one of the most powerful signs of feeling wanted; just as sexual rejection gives comparable pain. Coitus thus is a recurrent act

of faith, hope, and love in one another – independent of the physical and psychological outcome.

– Finally, it is one of the most powerful ways of saying "Thank you for being with me yesterday, today, and hopefully tomorrow." Apart from its pleasurable meaning, it is one of the most powerful transmitters of the I-Thou encounter and this happens independently of the frequency of the act which has become the obsessive preoccupation of the world.

Finally, separately from the total spiritual dimension of the sacrament, in Genesis we see intercourse recognised not only as good but *"very good"* (Gen 1:31). With the Song of Songs and with other passages, it becomes a sacred act. According to the Second Vatican Council, sexual intercourse is intimately linked with love and even the world talks about 'Let us make love.' John writes *"God is Love"* (1 Jn 4:8).

We can conclude from all this that sexual intercourse is a recurrent act of prayer – one of the most important in the life of the couple.

Ultimately coitus unites the couple physically, while remaining completely separate but related interpersonally through their love; united and yet separate while remaining one. That is my understanding of the Trinity and for me sexual intercourse is a powerful symbol of the Trinity.

I conclude this article by bringing to the attention of married couples that in the presence of this sacrament, their whole life is infiltrated with the presence of God. In combination with the Eucharist, it is the basis of their daily spirituality reflecting the image of God in this world and preparing them for their eternal destiny in the next.

The Theological Value of the Married Priesthood

Basilio Petrà

People's lives often follow unexpected and unforeseen paths that appear to be caused by chance or by the network of acquaintances and relationships that each person's activities create, and by the incalculable interaction in this network. I say "appear," because we subsequently glimpse a meaning that is not arbitrary nor linked to one specific occasion, a meaning that is premeditated and prepared. It is then that we perceive the action of Someone who goes ahead of us, the mystery of non-arbitrariness in which our life has its place.

Something like this happened to me too when I came into contact with INTAMS (International Academy for Marital Spirituality) and met so many people who were motivated by the *vision* of the spiritual meaning of conjugal experience in the sacramental context. I was struck by the profound conviction that guided them, namely, the conviction of a full harmony between the conjugal vocation and the vocation to the fullness of the Christian life, between the vocation to the total gift of oneself in conjugal love and the vocation to the total gift of oneself to the Lord Jesus in the Church.

As relationships deepened and our work in common increased, I came more and more to realize that I had, as it were, a special task assigned to me within INTAMS, that of *giving support to this conviction* by making present a reality that is characteristic of the Eastern Christian tradition, that is to say, the conjugal experience of married priests and of their wives. The Eastern ministry, including that of the Greek Catholic Church, is very largely a married ministry; in some churches, the parochial clergy are normally married.

Recalling the Existence of the Married Christian Priesthood

There has not been, either in the past or in the present, a conspiracy of silence with regard to the married Eastern clergy. Rather, it has simply been forgotten.

It has been forgotten in the ordinary Western perception of the priesthood, which has been thought of as always (and intrinsically) linked to celibacy. But it is much more relevant and important to note that it has also been forgotten in the theological and spiritual realm. When we read the texts published by the Roman curial congregations or other texts of the Roman magisterium, it is easy to see that whenever they speak of the theology of the priesthood, they have in mind only the celibate model; the same happens when these documents speak about priestly spirituality.

One peculiar sign of this forgetfulness is the dominant mental link whereby matrimonial spirituality is thought of and formulated as a spirituality proper to the layperson, that is to say, within the lay vocation. In the general Eastern tradition, including the Eastern Catholic traditions, nuptial spirituality is a spirituality that – precisely *qua* nuptial – is common to the laity and to the married ministerial priesthood. The differences lie not in the

nuptial experience, but in this experience as it is determined by a different task in the Church, by a different relationship to the mission and government of the Church: the priest is at the service of the Church in institutional terms as an *ordained minister* of the Church, while the layperson works according to his or her own ecclesial vocation in the world and in the Church.

As the East sees it, matrimony is not a part of the constitutional difference between the ordained priesthood and the laity. Rather, it designates the fundamental difference between the monastic and the non-monastic life, since monasticism is characterized by dying to the world. The monk flees from the world and dies to himself in order to live already the heavenly state of life, the *bios angelikos*.

Theoleptus of Philadelphia (†1322), the spiritual master of Gregory Palamas, the great theologian of hesychasm, sets out very clearly this intrinsic contradiction between the married life and the monastic profession in one of his texts: "Monastic profession is a tree with a lofty crown. It is very fruitful. Its roots are detachment from all bodily things; its branches are the impassibility of the soul and its refusal to have any kind of relationship with the earthly things from which it has fled; and its fruit is the possession of the virtues, the deifying love, and the joy that cannot be taken away from it" (*Discourse* 1.3).

The Precious Truth that is hidden and safeguarded in the Married Priesthood

Extricating the conjugal experience of the married priesthood from forgetfulness is much more than merely providing supplementary information. Since what I have said up to now may suggest this, let me attempt to express the matter more clearly.

Hidden in the intimate recesses of this forgotten reality, there is in fact a precious reality that must be brought to light, a truth that has been ignored or even denied so many times in the history of the Church and of its spirituality.

I refer to the truth that conjugal existence is completely compatible with the ministerial exercise of the ordained priesthood of Christ.

The meaning of this truth may become clearer if we bear in mind broader considerations.

There can be no doubt about the fact that in the Western tradition of the Church *today* the conjugal state is seen in its nobility and its positive character, and indeed in its very profound theological and sacramental value. Innumerable books and articles, courses and homilies spread far and wide the fascinating vision of nuptial love as an interpretative and explanatory model of the entire dispensation of salvation (God as the bridegroom of humanity, humanity called to the nuptials with God) and as a revelation of the love of Christ and of the Church. They proclaim the dignity of the family as an image of the Trinity!

The appeal has been made both in the recent past and in the present to contemporary personalism, in order to bring out the intimate relationship between subjectivity, otherness, communion, and union which characterizes the divine life, and which is found in the human experience of conjugal and family life ...

All this is indeed true and deserves the highest appreciation. It is not for nothing that the Church's magisterium has made its own this vision of matrimony.

At the same time, however, there is something in today's Western vision that must give us pause for reflection. No matter how noble conjugal existence may be, no matter how much it may be a *revelation* and an *icon* of the love of Christ, we are told that it

is nevertheless impossible to attribute it in any way as a form of existence to the individual person of Christ.

It is indeed true that this type of existence can be attributed to him in a symbolic and metaphorical form, that is to say, to him as the *spouse of the Church* (the *new humanity*), who gives himself so totally to the Church that he even purchases it with his blood. But it cannot be attributed to him as an individual person, as Jesus, the Messiah from Nazareth.

This is not simply a statement of facts, the historical observation that Jesus did not have this concrete type of human experience. It involves a fundamental affirmation: in Christ, we are told, conjugal existence and the sponsal (total) gift of himself to the Church are incompatible *in principle.* The latter ultimate gift of self excludes the former. It is as if they were essentially competitors.

Let me insist on this point: in the contemporary Western theology of matrimony, we are told, on the one hand, that matrimony makes visible the sponsal union between Christ and the Church – it is the sacrament of the love of Christ for the Church. On the other hand, we are told at the same time that conjugal existence is incompatible with the totality of the gift of oneself to the Church, since the conjugal gift of self, by its very nature, excludes the total gift of self to the Church.

This is stated very clearly in *Pastores dabo vobis* 29:

> It is especially important that the priest understands the theological motivation of the Church's law on celibacy. Inasmuch as it is a law, it expresses the Church's will, even before the will of the subject expressed by his readiness. But the will of the Church finds its ultimate motivation in the link between celibacy and sacred Ordination, which configures the priest to Jesus Christ the Head and Spouse of the Church. The Church, as the Spouse of Jesus Christ, wishes to be loved by the priest in the total and exclusive manner in which

> Jesus Christ her Head and Spouse loved her. Priestly celibacy, then, is the gift of self in and with Christ to his Church and expresses the priest's service to the Church in and with the Lord.

We are told here that the total love for the Church – the sacramental sign of which is given by the sacrament of matrimony – is incompatible with conjugal existence in the Church. To love the Church as Christ loved it competes not only with conjugal love in general (pre-sacramental love) but also with sacramental conjugal love itself, that is to say, the love that is animated by the Spirit of the Lord and is linked to a vocation in the Church and for the Church.

One cannot love the Church totally, and simultaneously build up a total and full human love in fidelity to an ecclesial calling. When *Pastores dabo vobis* says that the Church wishes to be loved by the ordained minister in the same way in which it is loved by Christ – that is to say, in a "total and exclusive manner" – it intends to affirm that conjugal love is essentially incompatible with the total manner (exclusiveness is one aspect of the totality) of love for the Church. This applies *only* to conjugal love, not to filial or fraternal love, not to the love of friends, not to the love of one's native land, of study, of art, and so on; all these loves have a powerful impact on the life of every priest.

No matter how one may wish to explain this matter, we are left with the statement that the two loves – for one's married partner or children and for the Church – cannot *simultaneously* be total. One who enters into matrimony is entering into a condition that essentially excludes the total gift of self to the Church. This means in concrete terms that the life of a Christian spouse, a life that is given to his wife, his children, and to the social network that is generated by the family, is a life that cannot coexist with the gift of self to the Church.

Christian conjugal life is a visible sign of the total love of Christ for the Church, but at the same time a condition of life that does not permit total love for the Church in the way that Christ loves it.

However, the Christian married priesthood, both Orthodox and Greek Catholic, attests that there was always an awareness in the Church as a whole that conjugal existence is completely compatible with the total gift of self to the Church, and that it does not *essentially* compete in any way with total love for the Church or with service of the Church.

A Conclusion

There is no human condition that prevents a Christian from exercising a total love for the Church, since, thanks to baptism, the existence of the Christian is already an *ecclesial existence,* as J. Zizioulas felicitously puts it. The ecclesiality enters into the essential structure of the Christian, since he or she now lives in Christ. Wherever one is placed in the Church or in the world, the Christian's own specific vocation calls one to live a life that is fully ecclesial, fully at the service of the Church which is the new humanity in Christ that is growing in history.

There is no "true" human love that implies for a Christian incompatibility with a total love for the Church – not even conjugal love.

Love for one's married partner (and children) and total love for the Church do not cancel one another out, nor are they mutually exclusive. They are not on the same level, just as love for one's partner and children and love for God are not on the same level. X. Thévenot has rightly said that "contrary to what a frequent spiritual illusion would have us believe, sexed love for God and sexed love for a human being do not belong to the same or-

der. The first love transfinalizes the second, revealing all that it implies" (*Dictionnaire de Spiritualité* XV, 777). The two loves do not belong to the same order. Their relationship is not that of quantitative entities that can be added or subtracted: both the love for God and the love for the Church, both the gift of self to God and the gift of self to the Church, live and are realized *through* human loves and *in* concrete human loves, without *necessarily* contradicting one another.

If conflicts arise between the two loves, this is for factual reasons, not for reasons of principle, because of limitations that are due to finitude or to personal guilt. And these are limits that affect everyone, whether we are married or single.

The Essential Necessity of Stickability

Elizabeth Davies

> Stickability: the ability to stick to a particularly hard job or trade, to hold on when losing, to stick to a task or situation, to stick with something until you perfect it (Urban Dictionary).

My mother always said that it was not enough to be born intelligent or talented, since the key to success was perseverance. Attentiveness, concentration, patience, tenacity, and the ability to stick to something – a piece of homework, a hobby, a sport, or a friendship – were some of the qualities of which she constantly reminded us, while she guided us through the ups and downs of childhood and adolescence. I will always be grateful to her for that.

Even today, the pain caused by unfulfilled expectations or by goals that I have failed to reach is usually assuaged by the comforting certainty that a new day begins tomorrow and there will be other possibilities and attempts to succeed at "it," no matter what "it" may be.

If, then, there is one quality that I would like to give my own children for their path through life, when they cross the gloomy relational waters of young adulthood in the search for a partner – and especially when they have found someone and then (as I

hope) decide to marry and to found a family – it would be this idea of stickability.

It has carried me through the difficult times of my own marriage. It has assured me that I have done my best even when things did not go well. And it has helped me to hold out even when that did not seem truly meaningful in the eyes of outsiders.

But before I continue, I must point out that hanging on is not without its dangers. Perseverance ought not to be recommended or practiced in a situation of abuse or danger. What I am interested in here is the broader application of stickability, its value, and its significance for healthy and life-giving relationships.

When I think of the adults who are genuinely important to me, those with whom I am linked by a personal relationship, I must say that although some relationships were easier than others, no relationship was really completely free of problems. One of the most difficult tasks that we must master is to live together with another person as a committed couple. We may perhaps feel more "at home" with our partner than, for example, with good friends or work colleagues, but we cannot escape the question who we are (or who our partner is), where we are coming from, and what is the goal towards which we are moving, either as individuals or together.

When we love someone – *truly* love him or her, so deeply and comprehensively that we cannot imagine life without this person – we cannot leave this relationship as soon as we are displeased by something that the other has done or has failed to do. What then can we do? An effort is required, if we are to regain the equilibrium and to restore peace between the partners. Sometimes, we grind our teeth as we resist the incipient self-pity, the impulse to utter reproaches, or the inner feeling of rejection. Determination is needed, in order to struggle to speak clearly with one another, and to understand and accept one's own inadequacies and to make

amends. Tenacity, perseverance, and dedication are needed, if one is to motivate oneself (and the other person) again and again each day to work one's way through imperfection, self-centeredness, thoughtlessness, and a lack of sensitivity. All these positive qualities are identical to the quality of stickability.

This may all sound very negative, precisely because of its great importance. But anyone who works professionally with the interaction between couples can confirm how strongly the negative affects human relationships. For example, the celebrated American psychologist and scientist John Gottmann has argued in detail that the mark of a marriage that can tolerate stress is a proportion of 80 to 20 between positive and negative exchanges. He affirms that each negative interaction requires at least four positive interactions, in order to regain the equilibrium in the relationship. Sometimes, even more may be needed.

My own marriage, which has not been good at tolerating stress, has compelled me to reflect long and deeply on these negative interactions, since it is so difficult to endure them. And it is all the more difficult when the volume of negative interactions is disproportionate to the positive interactions. Bad words and actions are a heavy burden. This means that I am acquainted with the power of the negative, and I fear it. On the other hand, this is precisely why I find stickability so important. It helps us through the trials and tribulations of conflicts, challenges, and crises, when our biochemistry might perhaps blur our judgment. In such cases, stickability helps us to endure at the place where reconciliation awaits us.

We are complex creatures. Intellectually, we are aware that we are the product of our genes and of our environment, and that almost every individual experience of relationship has left its mark on us and has prepared the way for the adventure of a lifelong love. What we have already grasped along our path can perhaps

be useful to us. But it may not in fact be truly helpful when we attempt to understand the other or to react appropriately to him or her.

In my own family, for example, my siblings and I regard the "cross fire" between our parents as something normal, but the deep devotion and thankfulness that they feel for each other after fifty-seven years of married life tend to remain hidden from outsiders. They have developed their own way of being together and their own language of love. Nevertheless, the fact that this functions for them certainly does not mean that this is true of other couples as well. The challenge remains, and one must test out many things, if one wants to find out what really functions. Stickability is especially important here.

When something has gone badly and I am misunderstood by the other, we must at some point simply stop and go back step by step in our dialogue, so that we can analyze where the misunderstanding arose and where reaction and counter-reaction have led us to take a new and unintended direction. This may be laborious and even painful, but it is a helpful and honest process.

In emotional terms, this does not always succeed, especially when things become really difficult in concrete situations. The impulse to fight or to flee, which is deeply rooted in our psyche, is activated. We know that stress triggers strong chemical reactions in our body, which were important for our survival in prehistoric times. But neither fighting nor fleeing opens up genuinely optimal possibilities, when we want to settle disagreements with our partner.

But what is the advantage of this stickability? What is the point of looking for solutions, when we can get out of each other's way or evade each other when differences of opinion arise? I wish to describe three concrete experiences here, although I could also present others. First of all, I have learnt a great deal through the

person whom I love. Secondly, I have learnt a great deal about myself and my abilities. Thirdly, I have discovered that it is quite simply worthwhile to hang on.

To begin with the other person: much of what we know is the result of positive experiences during the first phase of being in love, when romance reaches its high point and we see everything through rose-colored spectacles. We get to know the family and the friends of the other, his or her preferences and disinclinations, and all that we have in common. All of this is good and important. Often, however, the inevitable differences are not perceived for what they are at this early point in time. The things we have in common seem to us more important, more of a bond, and more relevant. We find the differences disturbing. But they do not cry out for our attention, whereas we enjoy the romantic feelings, and everything else is running so positively.

When the differences then emerge more clearly – and this is something that simply happens – this is often a shock. Is this person really what I thought he or she was? Have I made a mistake? Does the other think that he or she has been mistaken about me?

While we are carrying out this renewed assessment of the other, we are offered the wonderful possibility of really getting to know the other, perceiving him or her in a less idealized manner and coming closer to the person as he or she genuinely is. The struggle for reconciliation demands of us a certain measure of honesty, which is less urgent, as long as all is going well. This endeavor demands that both of us realize that we are anything but perfect. Fear of a potential loss now becomes a strong incentive to find a different kind of communication. It is not easy to face up to these unpleasant insights, but it proves to be both fascinating and helpful. The exposure of the vulnerability of our partner allows us to get to know the other far better and to develop a profound love.

At the same time, although it is a fact that we know our own

selves better than any other person, we cannot perceive and know our own selves in the same way as other people perceive and know us. Our own vanity or our own doubts can block our view for a time. Even when we ask others to describe us as they perceive us, it is all too easy for us to filter their reaction. It seems that only those who are closest to us, those whom we have known longest, are able to communicate the truth about us and also to support us in the task of becoming better people. What they think about us matters to us, and we want to become better for their sake. They speak about us in a tone of love, and they know exactly what we experience every day. They have accompanied us through the various phases and cycles of our life. And even if it is not easy, we can nevertheless accept their truth about us and get to work on ourselves for their sake. It is certainly not easy to change certain aspects of our personality, but our love for the other person, and our wish to maintain a good contact with him or her, are a strong force that works for our own good.

Ultimately, hanging on is worthwhile. The joy and satisfaction at having been together with the other for many years, and at having come through many difficult conversations, leave their mark on the couple and give them a solid shape *as* a couple. The transformations, the honest and loving exchange, and the satisfaction at being able to love and at being loved as one is, represent the fulfillment of our goals in life. Stickability creates here a perspective with fewer irritations, and ensures that important differences are accepted and that we pay attention to them. This is a task that never comes to an end, because we change in the course of the years. Something that is decisively important in one particular phase of our life may perhaps no longer be important in another phase. Stickability leads us through many storms, so that every single challenge deepens our understanding of each other and of

our own person, and confirms how unique we in fact are for the other.

I should like to conclude by noting that, in my opinion, stickability is a quality that develops quite naturally from the weakness and the vulnerability of a person who loves. It grows and becomes stronger with every challenge that is successfully mastered, but it ought never to be taken for granted. Our relationship survives in some phases thanks to our own stickability, and in other periods only thanks to the stickability of our partner. In the last analysis, both partners must hold fast to the relationship and assume responsibility for mastering the difficult task of reconciliation. Both partners must give and receive. This brings us to a deeper mutual understanding. And we can accept each other to the extent that is required, if we are to make the gift of our own self.

Married Life: A "Revolutionary Road"?

Elvira Roncalli and John Ries

> This was the way he had often wished his marriage could always be – unexcited, companionable, a mutual tenderness touched with romance – (Richard Yates, *Revolutionary Road*)

Do we not all have a picture of "married life"? Whether we are married or not, old or young, man or woman, we all seem to know what "married life" is supposed to be like. Perhaps, we have gained such a picture over time, by observing how married people are with one another: our parents, relatives, friends, or through images offered to us by books, movies and cultural beliefs in general; all of these, to various degrees, have conveyed something about "married life" that has made its way into the picture we hold. Perhaps we have elaborated this picture for ourselves, even embellished it, and have turned it into something like a model – a sort of ideal of a marital relationship – thereby becoming something toward which to strive, something by which to measure the success or failure of a marriage, depending on how closely it matches such a picture. Or perhaps, we have concluded that such a picture is just a relic of the past, corresponding to a reality that may have worked at some point in time, but that in the present, given how much has changed, no longer does.

Whether the picture of marital relationship we have come to hold is clear or obscure, it is however, relevant only to a point. The more relevant and crucial question is whether what we bring with us will enable us to develop an enduring and meaningful relationship, or whether it will turn into a hindrance that will stifle its life out of it. While it is inevitable that we do not start off *tabula rasa* – after all, who can escape the spell of tales' omnipresent final lines "and they lived happily ever after..."? – it is also indisputable that married life is no easy endeavor. The notion of "happy endless love," or of "a mutual tenderness touched with love" is, no doubt, very appealing, and we may wish to hold on to it whatever it takes, without, however, fully realizing what it really takes. So, what does it take?

In Richard Yates' novel *Revolutionary Road*,[1] April and Frank Wheeler, a young married couple starting out their life together in the 1950s, seem to have what it takes: they are bright, they are beautiful, they are talented and they are in love with one another. Everything about them is promising. What further sets them apart from other couples of their time, is their full awareness of being different, of not quite fitting in the mold of American suburban reality, of their deep dislike for the stifling conventionality of middle class life-style, something they perceive as decadent, rotten at the core and from which they wish to escape. The story unravels in unexpected ways, everything seems to turn against them; even they, at first bound together against the "hopeless emptiness of everything," later turning against one another, becoming each other's worst enemy and succumbing to the struggle. The love existing between them is rebuked: "... there's never been anything between us but contempt and distrust and a terrible sickly dependence on each other's weakness....and that is why I'll never again believe in anything you think, let alone in anything you say..."[2] in April's own words, at the end.

This is the story of how things have spiraled into something awfully wrong, when they could have just as well grown into something fruitful. The bitterness we are left with is reminiscent of a human tragedy; it is the taste of a promise not kept, of something deeply amiss. We replay the story in our mind endlessly, hoping to find the fatal turning point, the moment when, if we could grasp it, the worst could be spared. But in vain, it is right there, it unfolds before our eyes, in their words, in their choices, in their actions, yet it cannot be captured into one distinct moment. What we see, are a man and a woman desperately seeking to find each other, and failing miserably.

Is married life this hard? Is it doomed from the start, especially when veering off the given tracks of societal expectations and aspiring to ways of being lived out differently? Is it as ill-fated as April and Frank's charming house on Revolutionary Road?

These are fundamental questions and deserve to be taken seriously, especially in a time when enduring, genuinely committed relationships appear less and less likely. Can elements be distilled that lead toward a meaningful relationship rather than a failed one? In philosophical terms: what are the conditions for the possibility of a good and life-giving married life? Such conditions, however, cannot be purely formal; they must be lived day in day out, in the midst of heavy burdens and concrete constraints. Moreover, to raise this question about married life, involves raising the question about a certain modality of existence: a way of being most intimately and most concretely in relationship with another.

Married life is thoroughly enmeshed in the concrete: professional life, household life, children, finances, family and friends, even the place where it originates is not indifferent; everything has its weight and contributes to what married life comes to be. To work from some abstract ideal is tantamount to leaving behind that specific way of existence, to deserting it and taking refuge

in a purified version that may provide some respite, but which nonetheless distorts its reality. Married life is an incarnated reality with all the sinews of life that this entails. If we try to explain Frank and April's situation from an exclusively theoretical standpoint, we risk losing them altogether. Frank and April are not just "human," they are specifically and uniquely "Frank" and "April." If we neutralize who they are in the flesh, what each thinks, what each feels, what each does, we may as well not be talking about them at all. To see them exclusively through the lens of gender roles falls short, as well. Frank is a man who cannot fully escape the demands of masculinity imposed by the social norms of his time, (the bread-winner, the head of the household, the stern father...), yet, he is more than that. He is a man resisting becoming the man everybody tells him he should be, struggling to become who he is in himself and in relationship with April. Likewise, April is not simply struggling to conform to the social role of a housewife and mother, she is struggling to find herself in relationship with Frank.

Married life entails finding a way of being rooted in concreteness, but also a way of being most intimately in relationship with another. Here is where one risks losing oneself and the other, precisely when seeking to find oneself and the other. Here is also where it becomes apparent that the two in relationship are on their own, that they are blazing a new road, making a future come to be. Although, there are others who are married, they are on their own in shaping their life path together and give it their own expression. If married life is about transformation, then they must be truly "revolutionary": let go of all pre-given ideas, conceptions, not simply of "married life," but of each one himself/herself, in who each has come habituated to be. This is far from easy, it is a condition of perennial and genuine openness; one is always leaning outside of oneself towards the encounter with the other.

There is a paradox at the heart of this: given the deeply intimate character of the relationship, that which brings the two together and unites them, is also that which can separate them and tear them apart. The ease with which both April and Frank had been able to open up with one another, revealing to one another, one's own most secret thoughts, feelings and aspirations, had brought them intimately close and allowed them to be truly themselves. In Frank's own words: "You know what this is like, April? Talking like this? ... It's like coming out of a Cellophane bag. It's like having been encased in some kind of Cellophane for years without knowing, and suddenly breaking out ... I just felt this terrific sense of life, I felt so full of blood. Everything looked realer than real... this is really true – this is truth."[3] At the end of the book, however, what appeared "realer than real" and as "truth" has turned into a "treacherous thing," something that "once you started, it was terribly difficult to stop." In April's own words: "And all because, in a sentimentally lonely time long ago, she had found it easy and agreeable to believe whatever this one particular boy felt like saying and to repay him for the pleasure, by telling easy agreeable lies on her own, until each was saying what the other most wanted to hear, he: ‚I love you' and she: ‚really I mean it; you're the most interesting person I have ever met."[4] What had been perceived as "truth," had now turned into "lies." How could this be? From April's retrospective look, it would seem that there never was genuine openness between them, only deception. However, this final outlook does not do justice to the minute yet recurring instances where they appear to one another as a ray of light, a pale glimpse perhaps, but real nonetheless. How else would they have been able to entrust one another in beginning their journey together? One is not alone: this is both the blessing and the curse of married life, once it is embraced, the relationship cannot stand still.

To choose to become married to someone is the beginning of a journey of discovery, of unveiling the deepest self, of coming to grapple with the remotest parts of oneself, parts we may well wish not to see for ourselves, let alone open to another. But if it truly is a way of coming to be most intimately, and most concretely with another, there is no avoiding this, the other becomes the mirror of oneself, reflecting back to us, who we are in the same way as one becomes the mirror to the other, reflecting back who he/she is. In this reciprocal unveiling, one stands naked before the other, in a condition of extreme vulnerability. In a way, it is like jumping into an abyss: one is thrusting oneself completely into the arms of the other, without knowing with certainty that an embrace is waiting.

Here looms the same paradox again: it is through the unmaking of oneself, by stripping away the images, conceptions, facades one has taken on, that an authentic married life may spring forth. In this sense, it is a truly *revolutionary* road: it is not forged from without, and it is always undoing the patterns it has erected from within. The moment it settles on a way of being, it has been congealed, its life sucked out. The two are in relationship with one another exclusively in that modality, the relationship has become that modality, nothing else, the two find themselves as in a trap, only, they are their own captives, captives to the patterns they have erected between them, rather than becoming the person whose glimpses have been revealed to one another.

It is truly a daring journey to forge and endure, since, finding oneself in this condition of extreme vulnerability, entails the risk of loss. It also speaks of an openness that is excruciatingly difficult to maintain in and through the exigencies of day-to-day life. We are not always open toward the other, nor are we perennially alert and attentive to the other as we can be; sometimes we are oblivious and self-absorbed. This, however, is not what ultimately makes married life fragile, since commitment, stemming

out of the promise of mutual love in which married life is anchored, allows for continuity to subsist in the midst of varying degrees of involvement.

Rather, rejection and loss are truly at stake. If married life is a way of being most intimately and most concretely in relationship with another, if it entails unmaking and unveiling oneself, to come to be open and ever so vulnerable before the other, then it is an inherently perilous road. This is the journey wherein one finds oneself and the other, but it is at the same time where one can lose oneself and the other. Because of the intimacy at stake, loss of one inevitably entails loss of the other as well. There is never one single cause for why it turns out this way or that way. As already said, one looks in vain at April and Frank searching for the reason why things have turned out as they have. The story shows that their love for one another leads them to seek ways to shape their life together from within, they do not want to simply conform to some external pre-given image of married life; they seek instead to create life rather than abdicating life, they wish to be true to themselves and to one another and reject the married life their friends are settling into. Yet, on this journey, they fail and do so in and through their own making. At any moment something could happen to turn things around for the better; at every corner there are opportunities for redemption, but April and Frank no longer seem to be capable of seeing oneself and the other as the way toward salvation; on the contrary, they can only see the other as the source of their own alienation, their own rejection and their own loss.

To conclude from this that married life is therefore doomed to failure – as it does fail so miserably and so unquestionably for April and Frank – is not merely mistaken (miss – taken), but more importantly misses something at the heart of the story. The challenging instances of concrete life are not just happenings or

misfortunes along the way; they are opportunities that call April and Frank – and indeed all who seek out a life of marriage – to more than a revolutionary picture of marriage. Married life calls for a revolutionary way of being so that all the ups and downs, twists and turns, of the daily path can come to be moments of grace where new possibilities might come to be born, where each one may come be. Such a *revolutionary way of being*, however, is far from being easy and demands a mutuality of self-emptying and self-giving. Self-emptying creates an opening, a possibility for each to come to be in the empty space offered, for each to be received, embraced and cherished in who each is. But while necessary, such an opening is not enough. Each must give oneself to the opening, fully enter this place of promise along the way, with all the vulnerability and fragility that it inevitably entails. In the words of Simone Weil, this requires a special kind of loving attention wherein "The soul empties itself of all its own contents in order to receive into itself the being it is looking at, just as he is, in all his truth."[5]

In the end – or perhaps from the beginning through the end – the revolutionary road of self-emptying and self-giving marriage calls for faith, hope and love, being born along the way, again and again. Herein, its hope will not be so much some "thing" hoped for – not some promised land of "happily ever after" pictures – but rather a way becoming and travelling the road of marriage – a road of deep promise of tomorrow. Its faith will not be so much security in particular things, roles or constructs – cookie-cutter patterns and expectations – but rather a confidence in each other that gives birth to possibilities in and through self-emptying and self-giving; its love will not so much be some romantic feeling – a tenderness touched with romance – but a passionate, caring attentiveness to the other as a unique road is being given shape in and through a mutual life bonding journey.

Notes

[1] R. YATES: *Revolutionary Road*, New York: Vintage, 2008.
[2] Ibid. 319.
[3] Ibid. 136-137.
[4] Ibid. 320.
[5] S. WEIL: *Waiting for God*, transl. E. Craufurd, New York: Harper & Row, 1973, 115.

John Henry Newman on Marriage and Family Life as a School of Love

Donna Orsuto

The relationship between married couples and their celibate friends often leads to a mutually beneficial opportunity to reflect on the meaning of commitment and vocation in the respective ways of life. INTAMS (International Academy for Marital Spirituality) has done much to promote both bonds of friendship between married couples and celibates as well as profound academic studies on how these two ways of life mutually enrich one another. As a celibate person, this is what I have valued most from my personal experience with INTAMS and so I wanted my contribution to this volume to somehow reflect this.

In searching for a topic, I turned to the writings of Blessed John Henry Newman (1801-1890). At first glance, this might seem an odd choice, because marriage was not a key theme in his writings and some of what he wrote about it was misunderstood. Yet, the fact is that Newman had many married friends and from every indication, he learned much from them. Some of these friends may have helped to shape his understanding of love and mutuality as expressed in both marriage and celibacy. As an example, I would like to explore specifically the relationship between Newman and the family of his best friend from his Oxford

days, John William Bowden (1798-1844). [1] This will provide the context for analyzing two sermons where the theme of marriage as a school of love also emerges.

Newman and the Family of John William Bowden

Newman considered John William Bowden a "bosom friend." They shared the same birthday, February 21st, though Bowden was three years older than Newman. At Oxford, they worked together on various projects. Even after university, when their career paths diverged, the two kept in touch. When John Bowden married Elizabeth Swinburne in 1828, she also entered into Newman's circle of intimate friends. The Bowdens had four children: Marianne, Emily, John, and Charles Henry. Charles was Newman's godchild. Newman had close contact with the family, visiting regularly, especially during the grave illness of John William Bowden. Bowden's death in 1844 was a terrible blow for Newman. He wrote in his diary "I sobbed bitterly over his coffin."[2] After Bowden's death, Newman continued to keep in close contact with the family. Like Newman, Elizabeth Bowden and her four children decided to become Catholic. The two boys eventually entered the London Oratory. The correspondence between Elizabeth Bowden and Newman concerning the vocational choice of her daughter Marianne shows how involved Newman was with the family. Though Newman suggested that Marianne enter a more active religious order, in the end she decided to enter the Visitation Convent of Westbury in 1852. Newman was invited to preach at her religious profession on 12 January 1854. The unedited sermon, included in Newman's *Oratory Papers,* not only offers insights into Newman's ideas about virginity and the meaning of religious profession, but also includes some beautiful reflections into marriage.

In order to understand fully the sermon, it is helpful to first explain his relationship with Marianne. He had baptized her as a baby in the Church of England and had watched her grow up. A year after Newman became a Catholic, she also, at the age of fifteen, made a decision to follow his example. Newman was an "uncle" like figure in her life. It is no surprise that she is mentioned thirty times in Newman's letters and diaries (vol. XI-XVII).

Marriage, Celibacy and the "Lesson of the Marriage Ring"

What is of interest for this study is precisely what he says about the "lesson of the marriage ring" in her profession sermon. What Newman does in this sermon is to link "virginity *with*, rather than opposing it *to*, the fulfillment of human love in marriage."[3] Newman states:

> The very idea of matrimony is possession – whole possession – the husband's is the wife and no other's, and the wife is the husband's and none but his. This is to enter into the marriage bond, this is the force of the marriage vow, this is the lesson of the marriage ring.[4]

The marriage bond becomes for the couple the particular way that they move from fragmentation to harmony and integration. It is this "one central and supreme attachment" that is the key to their happiness. Newman sees the wedding ring as a powerful symbol of this bond. When the couple exchanges rings, it is a symbolic way of emphasizing their commitment to lifelong love and fidelity. Newman continues:

> Two mortal creatures of God, placed in this rough world, exposed to its many fortunes, destined to suffering and death, join hands, and give the faith to each other that each of them will love the other

> wholly unto death. Hence each is made for the other – each has possession of the other in a transcendent way; each loves the other better than anything else in the world, each is all in all to the other: each can confide in the other unreservedly, each is the other's irreversibly.[5]

Newman recognizes that human beings have a great intellectual and affective capacity that needs to be channeled. He insists though that what brings integration and wholeness in life is not to merely love the many, but to "have one central and supreme attachment, to which none other can be compared." As the "perfection of human nature," marriage, which is divinely ordained and thus is considered a sacrament, provides a natural way to express this desire and so come to fulfillment.

> Man has great capacities: he has an intellect, and a heart for many things; his nature is expansive, nor can you say how many things he can know, how many things he can love, but he must begin from some fixed points. It is by the law of nature, the happiness of everyone, man and woman, to have one central and supreme attachment, to which none other can be compared. An affection, one, mutual. Sovereign, unalterable, is earthly happiness and his earthly strength.[6]

The passionate and exclusive love, the expressions of mutual self surrender and possession, as expressed in marriage also have a message for those who are called to live a life of celibacy. Celibacy as mere asceticism or self denial leads to "melancholy, isolation and independence," and as such has nothing to do with the Gospel notion of virginity. We were "made for sympathy, for the interchange of love, for self-denial" for the sake of another. And so when Newman talks about celibacy, he sees it in terms of spousal love with Christ. His language becomes lyrical as he speaks of a Christian notion of celibacy, "it is to have Him ours

wholly, henceforth, and for ever – it is to be united to Him by an indissoluble tie – it is to be His, while He is ours . . . "[7]

Underlying Newman's teaching is the conviction that spousal love is what most characterizes God's relation with humanity. As Daniel Cere notes in his excellent article "Newman's Lesson of the Marriage Ring", "The path of the married and celibate illuminate each other. The celibate is called to a spousal relation with God. But the celibate's self surrender to God also reveals the new depths of mutual surrender to which the married are called. The binding loves of the domestic circle provide patterns for the intimate familial forms of ecclesial life which celibates must rediscover."[8]

Love of Relations and Friends

What exactly the celibate may learn from marriage and family life is beautifully developed in another sermon of Newman entitled, "Love of Relations and Friends", delivered in his Anglican years at St. Mary's in Oxford on the Feast of St. John the Evangelist.[9] It demonstrates Newman's conviction that through loving those around us, our relations and friends, we learn to love "the world at large." This sermon also includes a reflection on how marriage and family life are like a school of love that teach us how particular love and friendship with those around us lead to a more universal love.

Newman's sermon begins with the scripture passage "Beloved, let us love one another, for love is of God" (1 Jn 4:7). His point of departure is that Jesus had intimate friends, including St. John the Apostle, who in popular thought and by Newman, is considered both the Beloved Disciple and the author of the Gospel and the First Letter of John. For Newman, the fact that the Son of God had a close friend shows us "how entirely He was man"

and how there is nothing inconsistent with the fullness of Christian love and loving those around us. As the sermon unfolds, it becomes clear that in Newman's thought, close personal friendships are not inconsistent with or an obstacle to the fullness of Christian love, but, on the contrary, they are a necessary stepping stone. With Christ's example before him, Newman suggests that "the best preparation for loving the world at large, and loving it duly and wisely, is to cultivate an intimate friendship and affection towards those who are immediately around us." Underlying his thought is the conviction that Christian love begins with the particular and then expands to reach out to others.

For Newman, St. John, who is honoured above all for what he says about Christian love, did not begin "with some vast effort of loving on a large scale." As one of the few disciples who had "the unspeakable privilege of being the *friend of Christ,*" he was, in a certain sense "taught to love others" through his personal relationship with Christ. Newman explains that "first, his affection was concentrated, then it was expanded." It began with Christ, extended to His Mother, the Blessed Virgin Mary, and then stretched beyond boundaries. St. John is an exemplar, *par excellence*, of the transforming love of Christ. He is "a memorial and pattern of love, deep, contemplative, fervent, unruffled, unbounded."

Marriage and Family Life as a School of Love

In that same sermon, Newman shows how the movement from concentrated to expanded love is worked out in marriage and family life. His message is simple, yet profound: what happens in the home is a school of love that prepares us for a more profound love of God and others. Beginning from the conviction that grace builds on nature, Newman explains that, "to honor our parents is the first step towards honoring God, to love our brethren ac-

cording to the flesh, the first step towards considering all men our brethren. Hence our Lord says, we must become as little children, if we would be saved; we must become His Church, as men, what we were once in the small circle of our youthful homes." The domestic circle becomes the place where the bonds of intimacy and mutuality are nurtured.

Newman also suggests that an inbuilt asceticism is part of marriage and family life that guards against selfishness that is the opposite of charity. For example, by its very nature, marriage, where people of different tastes are "obliged by circumstances to live together, and mutually to accommodate to each other, their respective wishes and pursuits," leads to a natural "self denial" which is so necessary for cultivating Christian love. Those who have no bounds, who are "independent in worldly circumstances, who can do what they please and indulge the love of variety and the restless humours which many find attractive, can easily fall into selfishness." Under the influence of the Holy Spirit, what is learned naturally is transformed. "And so the love of our fellow Christians and of the world at large, ... is the love of kindred and friends in a fresh shape."

Conclusion

As a celibate, Newman had a gift for developing deep and long lasting friendships, including friendships with married couples and their families, as demonstrated by the example of the John Bowden family. As he commented to a reviewer in 1868 to thank him for a review of his *Verses:* "I have often been puzzled at myself, that I should be both particularly fond of being alone, and particularly fond of being with friends. Yet I know both the one and the other are true, though I cannot no more reconcile them than you can."[10] If you visit the Birmingham Oratory where he

lived from 1858-1890, you will see a wall lined with photographs of family and friends located just near where he celebrated Mass. This close proximity of these photographs with that altar suggests that Newman recognized that through his deep bond of communion with the Lord, he could reach out to those whom he loved.

In 1879, when Newman became a Cardinal he chose, as the motto to go on his coat of arms, the words *"Cor ad cor loquitur"* ("heart speaks to heart"). The words, originally from St. Francis de Sales (1567-1622), are an invitation to a personal communication that reaches the depths of the other, expressed in simplicity, without duplicity, rooted in love. This is the sort of communication that Newman proposes for our relations and friends. Newman was convinced that the circle will grow: "We are to begin with loving our relations and friends about us, and gradually to enlarge the circle of our affections, till it reaches all Christians and then all…" Newman learned this lesson from his married friends, and through his sermons, he has shared that message with us.

Notes

[1] "Newman and the family of John William Bowden", in: *Friends of Cardinal Newman Newsletter* (Christmas 2005), 3-7.

[2] J.H. NEWMAN: The *Letters and Diaries of John Henry Newman*, v. 10: *The Final Step: 1 November 1843 – 6 October 1845,* ed. F.J. McGrath, London: Oxford University Press, 2006, 343 (entry for December 15, 1844).

[3] See the introductory note of Placid Murray to "Newman's Oratory Papers no. 18" in *Newman the Oratorian: His Unpublished Oratory Papers*, ed. P. Murray, Dublin: Gill and Macmillan, 1969, 270. See also D. CERE: "Newman's ‚Lesson of the Marriage Ring'", in: *Louvain Studies* 22 (1997), 84. This article provides an excellent corrective to those who suggest that Newman has a negative view of marriage.

[4] *Newman the Oratorian*, 277.

[5] Ibid. 275.

[6] Ibid.

[7] Ibid. 277.
[8] D. CERE: "Newman's ‚Lesson of the Marriage Ring'", 84.
[9] J.H. NEWMAN: *Parochial and Plain Sermons*, v. II, 5, London: Rivingtons, 1902; unless indicated, all further quotations refer to this sermon ("Love of Relations and Friends").
[10] See H. TRISTRAM: *Newman and His Friends*, London: Bodley Head, 1933, 27; J. COULSON: "John Henry Newman: His Genius for Friendship", in: *Clergy Review* 62 (January 1997), 18-21.

Epilogue

Carlo Maria Cardinal Martini †

More than twenty years have now gone by since Aldegonde and Hubert Brenninkmeijer-Werhahn told me about their project of reflecting anew on marriage as a sacrament. The justification they offered was simple, but little attention had been paid to it up to that time. Until fairly recently, the father, the mother, or both parents had come to the end of their lives at the time when the children became adults; but today, the children marry or leave their parents' house, and the parents remain alone, perhaps in the hope of grandchildren, but also with the prospect of being together for another twenty or thirty years, in a manner that, for most of them, was hitherto unknown and unaccustomed. In concrete terms, this meant for the married couple that the time of their partnership was extended by at least twenty-five to thirty years. This new perspective entails new challenges, and an answer must be found to them in both pastoral and spiritual terms.

Accordingly, the newly founded INTAMS Academy (International Academy for Marital Spirituality) set to work to study marital spirituality and to investigate, by means of international and interdisciplinary studies, the relationship between the marriage partners, in such a way that justice would be done both to

the essence of marriage and to the contemporary situation and society.

At that time, I found this justification both plausible and interesting. I did what I could to support this initiative – although my expertise and my experience lay in a different field. Both of these are rather limited today, because of my age and my ill health, and I must therefore be content to write a few accompanying words to this book, although I would like to have written a longer contribution of my own.

Today, twenty years after that first encounter, and in view of the further development of INTAMS, I am conscious that the path that was taken is truly worthy of reflection. Scientists from the whole world, specialists in questions relating to marriage, universities and other institutions, and married people themselves have devoted intensive study to the problems in the course of these years. Marital spirituality is now no longer a theme only for a few specialists and theoreticians. It interests the entire Church. This is confirmed by the present book, to which my confrère, Cardinal Godfried Danneels, professors, celibates and married people have contributed – in order to represent the entire people of God, as it were.

The title of this anthology is itself interesting: "Close to our Hearts: Reflections on Marriage." This means that although these reflections and considerations are written on the basis of great professional competence, they express closeness and sympathy with this path of love and of the gift of self that is made by a man and a woman. They thereby underline the incontrovertible values of the sacrament of matrimony.

Recent studies, as these contributions show, have explored the dynamic character of the relationship between the marriage partners and have thus drawn attention to phases of development that allow us to look at the marital relationship from a different per-

spective. This brings the monogamous and intrinsically complex essence of marriage into a new light. It can be seen, from a historical perspective, that this is a specific element of the *humanum* and is a fruit of the Spirit.

The various transitions and stages of the lasting unity between husband and wife can now be seen more clearly. A greater clarity now attaches to the different purposes of marriage and to their reciprocal relationships. And this brings out all the more clearly the working of the Holy Spirit – for example, when the married partners persevere in friendship with one another, stand by one another, and above all, collaborate in their tasks of education and in the building up of a common organism that is a part of the divine plan.

It seems to me that it has been possible in this way to bring to light the stages of the Christian marriage that build upon one another, and yet are distinct. Bernard Lonergan emphasized these in an impressive article that he wrote in 1942: "Finality, Love, Marriage"[1]. This involves the transition from the sexual intimacy that follows a primarily generative purpose and is a part of the natural order for the conservation of the species, to the reciprocal and responsible help the partners give in the education of the children, in order in this way to lay the foundations for a profound friendship between husband and wife that lasts into the kingdom of heaven and is thus a part of the divine plan for humanity.

I feel a great respect when I see how out of this initial private initiative, with great dedication, conviction, and professional competence, a project has come into being that is, and should be, of benefit to the entire Church. This has given an example of how light can be shed on marriage with great intellectual openness and willingness to understand – while at the same time finding one's orientation in the Church's teaching, not least in order to be able to construct a solid and lasting foundation. In one sense, this col-

lection of essays marks the attainment of the goal of twenty years of intensive study and exchange, and of a solid experience. At the same time, it is an encouragement for all those who want to dedicate themselves to this task in the future. For as a matter of fact, the challenges remain great and serious, since we are aware of the complexity of the problems that face the family in God's plan of salvation.

Notes

[1] B. LONERGAN: "Finality, Love, Marriage", in: *Theological Studies* 4 (1943), 477-510; reprinted in his *Collection*, 2nd ed., repr., Toronto: Lonergan Research Institute of Regis College (Collected Works of Bernard Lonergan; 4), 1993, 17-52.

Janez Juhant, Bojan Žalec (Eds.)
Reconciliation
The Way of Healing and Growth

The book considers reconciliation from various points of view: biblical foundations of reconciliation, philosophical aspects, Girardian and Bonhoefferian reflections on reconciliation, intellectual and (post)totalitarian history, psychotherapeutic approaches ... The authors consider reconciliation also in very concrete (historical) contexts (Hungary, Russia, Slovenia, Islam and Christianity). Despite some disagreements, their common message is clear: human history and present times are covered with blood, suffering (of innocent victims) and negative emotions. Hence the only acceptable way is cultivation of the culture of reconciliation. Read the book to find out how.

Theologie Ost – West, vol. 16, 2012, 304 pp., 19,90 €, br., ISBN-CH 978-3-643-90202-3

LIT Verlag Berlin – Münster – Wien – Zürich – London
Auslieferung Deutschland / Österreich / Schweiz: siehe Impressumsseite

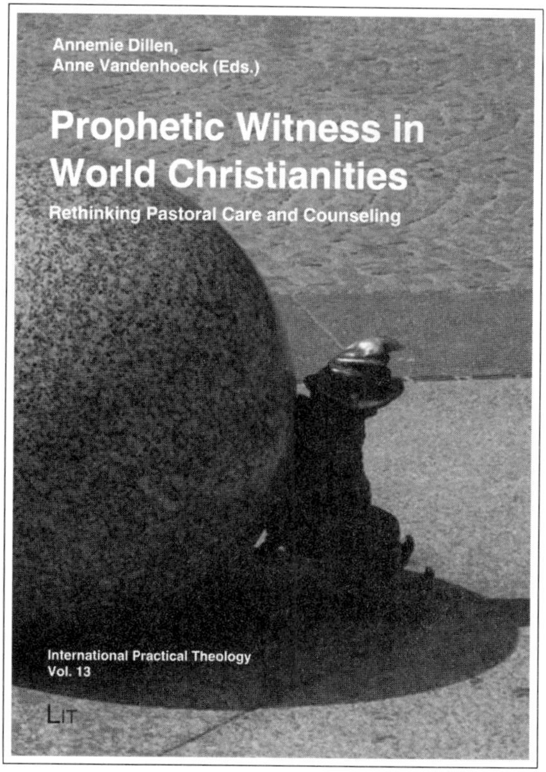

Annemie Dillen; Anne Vandenhoeck (Eds.)
Prophetic Witness in World Christianities
Rethinking Pastoral Care and Counseling
Prophets have a reputation of changing the relation between people and God for the better. Christianity has a long history of prophets who direct the faithful towards more justice and righteousness. What can Christians learn from prophets for daily life, for contemporary theology and pastoral care? This book undertakes the endeavor to look at prophetic acting from a biblical, pastoral and ethical perspective. The contributions of both, pastoral theologians and pastors from around the globe, make this study a unique exercise to keep the prophetic perspective in theological reflection and pastoral practice.
International Practical Theology, vol. 13, 2011, 248 pp., 24,90 €, br., ISBN-CH 978-3-643-90041-8

MEN UNDER THE GUIDANCE
OF REASON... DESIRE
NOTHING FOR THEMSELVES
WHICH THEY DO NOT ALSO
DESIRE FOR THE REST OF
SPINOZA
MANKIND...
R. Ruard Ganzevoort, Rein Brouwer, Bonnie Miller-McLemore (Eds.)
CITY OF DESIRES –
A PLACE FOR GOD?
Practical theological perspectives
LIT

SYMPOSION

Anstöße zur
interdisziplinären Verständigung
Towards an
Interdisciplinary Understanding

Band / Volume 12

LIT

Aldegonde Brenninkmeijer-Werhahn,
Klaus Demmer (eds.)

Close to our Hearts